www.susanschadtpress.com

Published in 2025 by Susan Schadt Press, L.L.C.

New Orleans

Copyright © 2025 Myra Menville

All rights reserved. No part of this publication may be reproduced, stored in any retrieval system or transmitted in any form or by any means, electronic, mechanical, photocopying or otherwise, without prior permission in writing from the publisher.

Although every precaution has been taken to verify the accuracy of the information contained herein, the author and publisher assume no responsibility for any errors or omissions.

No liability is assumed for damages that may result from the use of information contained within.

Design by Karya Mert

Library of Congress Control Number: 2024925809

ISBN: 979-8-9894034-7-9

Printed in the United States

And Then There Were Ten

Myra Menville

SUSAN SCHADT PRESS
New Orleans

Contents

Foreword — vi

Background — 9

Courtship and Marriage — 16

Calhoun Street — 22

Myra — 31

Kathleen — 41

Babydoll — 49

Dave — 59

Mimi — 65

George	73
Walmsley	81
Tom	87
Janet	93
Adele	99
Howard Black	107
Prologue	110
Appendix	cxiii

Foreword

Myra Semmes Walmsley ("Mere") was raised in a home whose occupants enjoyed generational wealth, superior education, political strength, and social prominence. She met and married David Carton Loker ("Pere"), a genteel man from St. Louis, and the two of them formed an unbreakable bond of love. Together they weathered the Depression of 1929 and raised ten children. The children were given a solid moral foundation of character, inner strength, honor, and respect. These children were quite different in personality but identical in their unwavering love and loyalty to one another. That bond that united them is the basis of this book.

This is the story of the Loker family, their success and failures, and their undying love of family. Each one found his niche in contributing to his community. The first family reunion of this branch of the Loker family reunion was held on Memorial Day weekend of 2005. After the devastation of Hurricane Katrina three months later, there seemed an even greater need to record information and share family histories. And so the idea of this book was formed.

Foreword

I am proud of my heritage as a member of this family. I want to tell the Loker family story and preserve it for the future generations in New Orleans and elsewhere. The information was given to me through written questionnaires, biographies from first generations, and oral histories. The accuracy is based on that information. I make no judgments and stand in awe of the genuine feelings expressed by all of the participants in this project.

I would like to thank those who were instrumental in either gathering information or typing the production of this book. I am indebted to Caroline and Angela Noya and Jane Ogden, who have successfully translated my scribble into countless pages of manuscript. I would also like to thank Karen Laborde and Judy Palmer, both published writers, who served as my editors. Without their assistance, this book would never have gotten to the final draft. I would be remiss if I did not mention Semmes Favrot, one of the family genealogists and historians, who is not only responsible for documenting the Loker and Walmsley chapter and updating the family tree, but he was extremely helpful in proofing this book. He is also responsible for writing the appendix. Beau Loker also contributed information on the Loker family.

I would also like to give kudos to the book committee: Wes Ancira, Mimi Finley, Billy Hughs, Caroline Noya, Helen McMillian, and me (Myra Menville). We have formed a special bond that makes us proud of our family heritage.

Last but not least, I would like to thank my granddaughter, Ainsley Grace Ancira, who typed the revised final draft of this book.

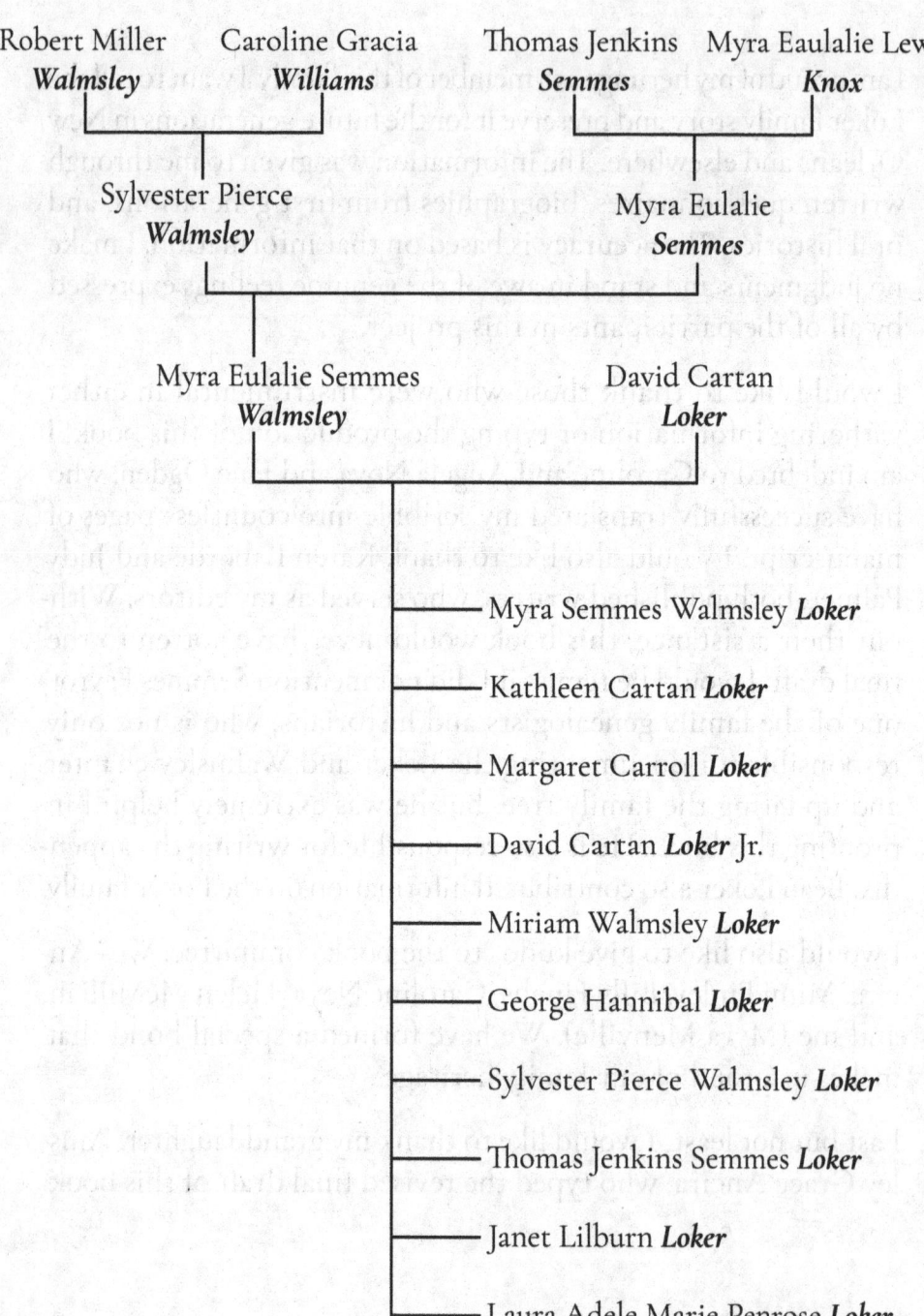

Background

Myra Eulalie Knox ("Myra I") was born in 1831 in Winchester, Tennessee, to Anna Octavia Lewis and Willaim Knox, an Irish immigrant. He started the Central Bank of Alabama, and it was his bank that first loaned money to the Confederate government. However, when the Civil War ended, he went bankrupt as a result. Myra was methodist and known for her philanthropic endeavors. Myra met her future husband, Thomas Jenkins Semmes, at Georgetown University. They were married in Montgomery, Alabama, on January 8, 1850, at Knox Hall, her father's home.

"It was while dancing the lances in a ballroom in old Georgetown, then the social capital of the nation, that the vivacious Myra Knox of Alabama first met her dashing Thomas Semmes of Washington." They moved to New Orleans and built a magnificent home on Annunciation Street in the lower Garden District. He was serving as Attorney General of Louisiana when the Civil War started. He supported secession as a delegate to the

Louisiana Secession Convention, and in 1862, he was appointed Confederate Senator for Louisiana. They spent the rest of the war living in the Confederate Capital in Richmond, Virginia, where they lived across the street from President Jefferson Davis and the Confederate White House.

While in Richmond and after New Orleans fell to Federal forces in April 1862, the Federal authorities seized their home in New Orleans due to his role in the Confederate government. The Irish servants watching their home passed all of the silver and other valuables through a back gate to keep the items from confiscation. After the war, the items were returned to the Semmeses, and it is said that not one item went missing.

In the spring of 1865, Mrs. Semmes (Myra I) was called to tend to four-year-old Joe Davis, son of Confederate President Davis, who had fallen thirty feet from a balcony while his parents were away from the home. Mrs. Semmes cradled the dying child in her arms until he died of his wounds. Myra had eight children of her own.

Returning to New Orleans after the war and after securing a pardon from President Andrew Jackson, Thomas Semmes sued the federal government for the return of his seized Annunciation Street home. After years of litigation, the U.S. Supreme Court finally ordered the return of the home. The Semmeses moved to a home on Iberville Street right off North Rampart Street at the edge of the French Quarter. They eventually settled in a home on South Rampart Street where one of their neighbors included author Grace King.

Myra died at the age of ninety-six in 1928, the "last surviving member of the first family of the Confederacy."

Caroline Gracia Williams has been labeled a "one-lady dynasty." It has been said that "as a queen, her throne was philanthropy and whose scepter, benevolence." Caroline was actually lovable and kind and known for her boundless charity, beautiful hospitality, and a gracious heart. She was one of the founders of the Christians Women's Exchange and served as their second president. She was on the board of the Louisiana Historical Society in 1895. She also founded the Quarante Club, a women's literary club promoting women authors. She served on that board from 1882 to 1905. Caroline died suddenly in Essex, New York, in 1905.

In 1856, she married Robert Miller Walmsley (1833–1919), an Episcopalian from Maryland. He was affectionately called "grandfather Walmsley." They lived on 1313 First Street in New Orleans. He was president of the New Orleans Clearing House, president of the New Orleans Board of Liquidation, and a prominent realtor. He was president of the Louisiana Cotton Exchange in 1880. After the Civil War, the Cotton Exchange was considered "the southern stock market." He received the Times-Picayune Loving Cup in 1912. He was president of the bank and served on the Tulane University Board. He was also a member of the Pickwick and Louisiana Clubs. T.J. Semmes and R.M. Walmsley were very close friends. Each had a child who respectively met and fell in love. They were married in 1885. Myra Semmes ("Myra II") was the daughter of Thomas Jenkins Semmes. Sylvester Pierce Walmsley was the son of Robert Miller Walmsley.

Myra II made her debut in 1885 and was a maid in Proteus and Maumus balls. She married Sylvester Pierce Walmsley on November 18, 1885. Sylvester Pierce was president of the Louisiana Cotton Exchange (like his father), first president of the Southern Athletic Club, and vice president of the Louisiana National Bank. They lived in the Semmes home on Rampart Street before residing at their Prytania Street home. One day, the couple were taking a buggy ride when Myra II was given the key to the house on 2507 Prytania as a wedding present. S.P. was captain of Comus for 27 years. He was asked to reign as Rex in 1890 and Comus in 1894. They had a happy and extremely privileged life together until S.P (Papoo) died in 1930. They had thirteen children together, eight boys and five girls. Two of the boys died as infants. One girl, Miriam, died at fifteen years old in 1919. Newspaper articles made a reference to a "Supper dance" that was held in honor of her sister Lucille that was postponed on January 7, 1919, due to "illness in the family" and another to sister Lucille being "now in deep mourning." Oral history says, "Miriam rode in an open carriage in cold weather to a ball in New Orleans, where she was to be presented at the Jerusalem Temple." It ended up being the coldest night of the year. She was not warmly dressed and contracted pneumonia and died in a week. Her mother, Myra II, was so distraught at her death that she never got over it and could not bear to hear the name Miriam spoken.

Myra II, affectionately called "mouse" by her mother because she was four foot eleven, died in 1960 at the age of ninety-four. She was called "Mamee" by succeeding generations. Papoo died in 1930.

Background

Robert Miller Walmsley and wife Caroline Gracia Williams

Myra Eulalie Knox Semmes (Myra I)

Myra Eulalie Knox Semmes and grandson Sylvester Pierce Walmsley, Jr.

Thomas Jenkins Semmes

And Then There Were Ten

Myra Eulalie Semmes (Myra II) and Sylvester Pierce Walmsley

Myra Eulalie Semmes Walmsley ("Mamee," Myra II)

Sylvester Pierce Walmsley ("Papoo")

Background

2507 Prytania Street (House of Mr. and Mrs. Sylvester P. Walmsley)

1313 First Street (House of Mr. and Mrs. Robert M. Walmsley)

Courtship and Marriage

Myra Semmes Walmsley Loker (Myra III), daughter of Myra Semmes and Sylvester Pierce Walmsley, was a strikingly beautiful woman with crystal blue eyes and a velvet, fair complexion. Although she came from a family of thirteen, she lacked nothing. She excelled at Georgetown Visitation Convent and later in life often told her grandchildren that she did not understand why all young ladies did not attend such a fine school. She failed to comprehend the necessity of the combination of brains and money.

The Walmsley house on Prytania and Second Street was three stories. The oldest uncle, Uncle Pierce Walmsley, and his wife Stella and their two sons Pierce and Phillip, lived on the third floor. They were called Uncle P. and Aunt Tee. Mere and Pere lived on the second floor. Myra, Kathleen, and Babydoll slept on the wide front porch, rain or shine, winter and summer. Mosquito nets were used in the summer because there were no screens on the porch. (Yes, the thought of children running around an

Courtship and Marriage

unscreened porch is scary, but they all survived.) Mamee (Myra II) had double parlors where chaperoned dances were held, hosting as many as two hundred fifty guests. With such a crowd, the temperature and humidity made the rooms excessively warm. It was not uncommon to see men carrying an extra shirt to change into if they were too hot. The band never played past one a.m., but right before it was to end, Mamee would come in with a sign that read, "And to all . . . Goodnight."

The dining room table was usually set for thirty people. Meals for the children were usually served on the porch. When one of the uncles wasn't going to be home for dinner, one of the children was allowed to eat at the main dining table. They were expected to be on their best behavior . . . finger bowls were served with a lemon slice and/or a rose petal. Dinners at Mamee's usually served thirty or more people and always at seven p.m. sharp. Papoo's house employed a staff of eleven servants. There were two cooks in the kitchen and a butler to serve the meals. Three women washed and ironed clothes all day. There was an upstairs and downstairs maid and Sophie the seamstress. Sophie was a tiny lady who sat at the end of the long second-floor hall. She came in at eight a.m. and left at five-thirty p.m. She took the streetcar home below Canal Street to Esplanade and never missed a day of work.

In those days, it was not uncommon to have pre-arranged marriages. And so it was that Myra III came to be engaged to one of the Gettys, who was a friend of her father S.P. Walmsley. Mrs. Laura Gore invited young Myra to attend the Veil of Prophets

Ball in St. Louis, and so she begged her father for permission. During her stay, there was a dinner party given in her honor, and her escort was David Carton Loker, who later became her husband. Infatuated with David, she phoned home to tell her parents that she was staying a few more days. Smitten, she returned home and broke her engagement to Getty. (Without that decision, none of us would be here and there would be no book.) She became engaged to David at twenty-two and lived at home until the wedding. David, who could not afford to come to New Orleans prior to the wedding, stayed in St. Louis.

David was distinguished looking and came from the Charles Flemming Loker family of St. Louis, "a perfectly lovely family." David stayed in his hometown exactly one year to work and save money for the marriage. He arrived in New Orleans the day before the wedding, which was celebrated November 18, 1911, at the Immaculate Conception Church. There is very little written about the wedding, but knowing of Mamee and Papoo's lifestyle, one can assume it was glorious.

Mere did not have the same festive engagement experience as her mother, but she did get pregnant on her honeymoon. After the honeymoon and on the way to St. Louis, Pere did not have enough money for both of them to eat and take a taxi from the train station to their home. It was not uncommon for women in those days to receive monthly financial help from their parents in the beginning of the marriage. Mere wrote home for supplemental help from her father. Daughter Myra IV was born nine months after the honeymoon, Kathleen came sixteen months later, and Babydoll eleven months after that. In 1917 when Babydoll was five months old, Mere wrote to her sister Carrie about her bleak arrangements in a third-floor walk-up with three young children and no money. Concerned, Carrie called her father and explained Mere's plight. Papoo immediately took the train to St. Louis to evaluate the situation for himself. Concerned, he insisted everyone get packed and that they were all to live with him and Mamee.

Everyone struggled financially, but one thing was certain: both Mere and Pere were deeply in love. Papoo tried to set him up in several businesses over time, but with little success.

It has been said that one evening at dinner in Mamee and Papoo's home, one of the uncles berated David about his work ethic and not contributing his share. Pere was heartbroken and never ate at their dining table again. All his meals were served upstairs.

And Then There Were Ten

David Cartan Loker ("Pere")

Myra Eulalie Semmes Walmsley (Myra III) Queen of Comus 1908

Myra Eulalie Semmes Walmsley Loker ("Mere," Myra III)

Myra Eulalie Semmes Walmsley Loker ("Mere," center) with her children (top right to left) Myra, Kathleen, Dave, and Peggy ("Babydoll")

Courtship and Marriage

And Then There Were Ten

Calhoun Street

Mere and Pere, with Myra, Kathleen, Babydoll, Dave, and Mimi, left the luxurious Prytania Street home and moved to 1722 Calhoun Street, a six-bedroom house across from Holy Name School. By then, Pere was in the insurance business thanks to Papoo's contacts. On a good day when business was brisk, Pere would bring home as much as $400 on a Saturday. Four hundred dollars was a lot of money at that time. Although business was not always that good, he made enough to support ten children and Virginie, daughter of Sophie the seamstress. Virginie washed clothes on a board, ironed, and cooked for only $1 a day. (Imagine!)

As much as Pere struggled financially, he was a huge success as a father and a family man. Pere never owned a car because they sold for just under $600, which was out of his reach. Roads during the Depression were terrible and unpaved. Mere and Pere walked everywhere. Pere became a daily communicant, living so close to

Holy Name Church. He wore a coat and tie to the dinner table every night, and after dinner he never left the house at night.

When the children were little, Pere would assemble them by calling each child by name and asking them to state their ice cream preference: chocolate, vanilla, or strawberry. A call to the Cloverland Dairy was made, and twelve Dixie cups were delivered in dry ice by a boy on a bicycle, who got a nickel tip for this trouble. The bent top of the ice cream cup, which was only two cents, served as a spoon. Sometimes, wooden spoons would be included in the order.

The Lokers had a wonderful home life. The boys gave Mere no trouble at all. Walmsley, Tom, and Dave (affectionately called Brother) played football. Tom, with his curly black hair, was a rascal. He could consume a loaf of bread, peanut butter, and a quart of milk before dinner. And Walmsley lived off a jar of peanut butter a day.

Mere wanted her girls to meet nice people and enjoy some of the privileges to which she had become accustomed. She insisted Pere join the Twelfth Night, Revelers Carnival Organization, so the girls could be presented in the Court. Although Pere was a member of that organization, he never went to see any of his children in the Court. Since he was not a native of New Orleans, he had no appreciation for the local customs.

There were plenty of people within the family to play with and no need to go anywhere. However, in the summer, the family would take the train to Hammond to pick strawberries. The trains then were only two to three cars. Mamee and Papoo also had a home in Pass Christian. There were only a few public pools in New Orleans, but Mere would not let her children go to any of them to swim. Since people did not swim much, except on the coast. Papoo's home on the coast became a water sport refuge. This house was later destroyed by Hurricane Camille in 1969.

Since Mere was raised with servants, she did not know how to cook. Pere, however, loved to cook and even taught Mere how to make gumbo. Pere was the permissive one and spoiled the children. He loved Hershey bars, and when the children would come home from school, there would be pieces of Hershey bars and a piece of fruit waiting on the mantle. He also stoked the fireplaces early every morning so no one woke up to a cold room. At Christmastime, the children never saw the decorated tree before Christmas morning. Socks were hung by the chimney for Santa to fill. Mere lined up the children so that they would sing a song before going to see their presents. The tree touched the eighteen-foot ceiling. Mere and Pere stayed up all night until the tree was decorated and all the toys were assembled.

Mere was the strict one and in the early days of raising children revealed her temper. When she could not find her stockings, she would wake up the older girls to help her find them. She often used her wire hair brush to spank those who needed correcting. It was safe to assume that living with ten children in tight quarters, little to no money, and surviving the Depression would put anyone on edge. By the time her children were grown, Mere's temper had mellowed and only her pure heart and loving spirit showed 'til the day she died.

As the girls got older and started going out on dates, they were never given a key to the house. They never really needed one because Pere was always there to open the door, which could be a good thing if you were trying to get rid of your date.

One of Pere's jobs was real estate. Mere's brother, Semmes Walmsley, was mayor of New Orleans from July 1929 to June 1936. Because of Pere's ties to Mayor Walmsley, Huey Long, then the arch enemy of the mayor, got on the radio and said that David Loker was an embezzler. This, of course, was a lie. Eventually, Long revoked Pere's real estate license as a political vendetta. Later, Pere suffered from a heart attack and was forced to retire, following the doctor's orders.

He spent the last years of his life with more time to spend with his children, especially the youngest ones. Adele, the youngest of the ten children, remembered walking to the Prytania Theatre from Calhoun Street with her father, who was dressed in his suit, tie, hat, and walking cane, to see his first and only movie, My Wild Irish Rose. Although he enjoyed the movie, he never went to another one. Pere lived for thirty-four years in New Orleans until he died at the age of sixty-eight of heart trouble. Pere died in Mere's arms, dying as he lived: close to her. Mere only wore black in the winter and white in the summer for two years, still grieving the man she loved.

Mere loved to walk. In fact, she had no problem walking from Calhoun Street to Canal and back. She would stop at the Louisiana Avenue K + B drugstore to have some ice cream and a rest. She also loved to shop at D. H. Holmes and would stop in their dining room for more ice cream, or soup if it was cold. She used the escalator because she was frightened of elevators. After shopping, she would walk back down Carondelet Street to Lee Circle, up St. Charles Avenue to Louisiana Avenue. She stopped at both K + Bs for more ice cream on the way before returning home.

It has been said that Mere got stuck in an elevator for hours when she was queen of Comus. Her claustrophobia stemmed from this terrible incident. She also would never put both arms in a coat at the same time. Mere would not ride in a car unless she held the door partially open. If she felt particularly nervous, she would open the car door and walk over to the sidewalk. Fortunately, John Menville (Myra IV's husband) gave Mere an anti-anxiety shot, and she gradually overcame her nervousness. He also convinced her to ride in a car with the door closed.

Mere was a woman of incredible strength, always interested in what everyone was doing, never focusing on herself. She had the world at her feet as a young lady, and as a woman, she had the love of her life with whom she raised ten children. One of her passions was genealogy. She spent her later days writing to people, hopefully relatives, all over the world. She donned a Comus Crown in 1908 and wore her son's football sweaters in her middle years. She was supported all her life—first by her father, then her husband, and later by various family members. And at no time did she ever waiver from the remarkable lady she had become. She never complained. As independent as she was, she ended up living for a few years with her daughter, Janet, giving her granddaughter the role modeling and love that little Janet so desperately needed.

Mere is most remembered as soft-spoken by her grandchildren, sitting in a big chair, with her lovely, wavy, snow white hair that she wore in a bun, a big smile, and an even bigger heart. On Sundays, she would hold court. Family members would pay a visit with all the offspring in tow. In between family visits, Mere spent most days entrenched in her genealogy, tracking the family tree practically back to Noah. It was easy to give her birthday and Christmas presents—all she wanted was stamps and stationery. She tried sharing her findings with all the younger generation, but it fell on deaf ears with the exception of a handful of enthusiasts. She was relentless, hoping some of the information would sink in through osmosis. Her writings are distinguishable through her beautiful handwriting.

Mere died on October 5, 1979, basically of old age. She had survived throat cancer and cervical cancer, which she contracted a few years before her death. The cancer was so slow growing at her age that Dr. Homer Dupuy said there was not much that could or should be done. It is the opinion of this author that she probably died of a broken heart and just gave up. She had buried so many people she loved in her lifetime—siblings, parents, husband, her adopted son, Howard, and so many friends. In November 1978, she buried her grandson, Jay Menville, who was murdered. Four months later, she buried his mother, Mere's firstborn. Myra (IV) Menville died of ovarian cancer at the age of sixty-six. Mere told Myra's daughter, with tears in her eyes (which was a miracle because she never cried), that she never expected to bury her own child. It seemed that eight months later, she let go of her very full life. She was tired and wanted to be with her "old man" as she so affectionately called Pere.

Ever since Mere died, things have been different. She was the glue in the family, and the family has never been the same since.

Calhoun Street

And Then There Were Ten

Myra Walmsley Loker Menville (Myra IV)

Myra

All of the Lokers were a good-looking group, but Myra IV was the uncontested beauty. Siblings, friends, acquaintances, and strangers are in agreement, and forty-five years after her death, people still comment on her looks. Myra Semmes Walmsley Loker Menville, the oldest of ten siblings, was born August 16, 1912. She was tall and slender with green eyes, wavy chestnut hair, and fair complexion. When Myra was three years old, her father was struggling financially. Mere's parents Mamee and Papoo arranged for her, Kathleen, and Peggy (nicknamed Babydoll) to live with them at their 2507 Prytania Street Home.

It has been said that Myra took advantage of her looks and enjoyed playing the actress. She adored Mary Pickford, the young Roaring 20s movie star of that day, and mimicked her by draping material all over herself, pretending to be a star-gazed actress. She would make scrap books of all the more popular movie stars. Later, Myra and Kathleen played well together, but sometimes

Myra did not want sister Peggy to play because she was younger. Mere insisted that Babydoll be allowed to play with her sisters, so Myra agreed. But not to be outdone, she informed Babydoll that they were playing house and that she could be the maid, and "it was her day off."

When Myra wore a bathing suit in her twenties, she could double for actress Dorothy Lamour. In addition to being a drama queen, Myra was used to having her way. On the third floor of the Prytania Street house, Mamee built closets the length of the hallway for storage, so Myra convinced Mamee to give her a closet of her very own. Myra also persuaded Mere to give her a room of her own, while Kathleen and Babydoll had to share.

In grammar school, Myra went to Miss Edith Aiken School (now Trinity Episcopal School). In high school, she attended the Academy of the Sacred Heart and, later, Grand Coteau, a private Sacred Heart girls school, in Sunset, Louisiana. Because of her beautiful face and flowing hair, she was usually chosen to crown the Blessed Virgin Mary at Sacred Heart. Later in her teens, she developed a goiter, which lasted for several years. The doctors told Mere that a cure was to wear a strand of pearls tightly around the neck. With Papoo's help, Mere bought Myra a cultured pearl necklace. This became a source of resentment for her sisters. The goiter eventually went away, with no help from the pearls, and probably with help from a little iodine in the food since goiters are closely connected to thyroid problems. Myra wanted to make sure that if she did pass on this problem to her children, she would provide a more reasonable remedy than a pearl necklace. She was told that fish eyes were a wonderful source of iodine. So when her children were young, she would cut up the eye of the fish and make them eat it. Fortunately for her children, Myra and Jay, iodized salt became available in the grocery store and fish dinners no longer included eyes.

Myra's hair fell to her waist, and every time she leaned over the tub to wash it, she fainted. So Mere would periodically send her to the beauty parlor to have her hair washed. She wore beautifully plaited braids on top of her head or in a bun held together with long hair pins. This childhood condition allowed Myra to do little housework, and Kathleen and Babydoll were asked to absorb their sister's share of chores. As the workload increased, so did their resentment. With this extra time on her hands, Myra became a voracious reader and, later, a writer. At the onset of the Depression, however, there was no money for Myra to go to college. The little money there was went to her four brothers' education. In those days, it was considered more important to educate males before females. Still, Myra had done well in school and had received a partial scholarship to Georgetown Visitation Convent. Unfortunately, there was no provision for books, travel expenses, or lodging, so she had to decline the scholarship. Myra always resented the fact that she could not continue her education.

With ten children, Mere and Pere had no money to finance college for Myra, much less a debut. But in 1932, their oldest child did just that, made possible with the income she earned at D. H. Holmes Department Store and help from her Aunt Dorothy

Walmsley, who bought all of Myra's clothes for the parties and Carnival Balls. Myra appeared as a maid in the Carnival courts of Comus (Papoo was Captain), Mithras, Twelfth Night, Mystic, and Athenians. Family background alone seemed to be sufficient criteria to make one's debut.

The Depression days forced everyone to work, and Myra left home to go to New York for employment. She stayed at the Barbizon Plaza where men were not allowed above the first floor. Again, her looks served her well. She modeled for Saks Fifth Avenue and for Vogue, sending home monthly checks to her family. She also traveled for Vogue magazine, helping to open offices all over the country. Fascinated by the arts, she hung around writers, artists, and musicians. Although she was an introvert, this New York Experience made her independent. Syndicated columnist Walter Winchell wrote that "Myra Loker was one of the ten most beautiful women he had ever seen in the United States."

Taken with the fast New York lifestyle, Myra finally decided to cut her beautiful hair. On her next visit to New Orleans, she chose to wear a hat, hoping to conceal her crime. Myra's place at the dining room table was seated right next to Pere. When Pere saw his daughter, he was more than upset—he was mad and did not speak to her for three days. At the table, he would ask any other child to pass him something, even if it was directly in front of Myra. After the three days, he broke his silence but never really got over it.

Several years later, Myra returned home for another visit, and she was photographed for the Society Section of the States-Item newspaper. John Gilmer Menville, a young doctor and Tulane graduate, saw Myra's picture in the paper. Since John knew her uncle, Semmes Walmsley, the mayor, he asked to be introduced to Myra. John was a handsome young bachelor practicing urology in New Orleans. They fell in love, and after a five-month engagement, they were married May 6, 1939. Myra abandoned her career to become a housewife and mother.

John Jr., called Jay, was born almost a year after the wedding, June 4, 1940. Shortly afterward, the navy shipped John overseas to New Guinea. He served the next four years as a captain and doctor in World War II. During the war, Myra IV would trade sugar rations for tobacco, and she and her good friend Bell Baudan would sit on the front porch smoking John's pipes. After John returned home in 1944, Myra had four miscarriages. John sent her to the Mayo Clinic to be checked, and after numerous tests, she returned to New Orleans. Her daughter, Myra V, was born May 21, 1947.

Myra was so thrilled to have Myra V. However, Mere on viewing Myra V at the hospital suggested that her daughter stay a couple of extra days: "Hopefully the child's looks would improve." Myra adored her children and was a good mother but very strict. She treated them a lot like her siblings. It is not clear whether her overprotectiveness was the result of having four miscarriages or just her need for control. Her daughter writes, "Thank God I had Aunt Kitty to stick up for me . . . she was always talking to Mom, convincing her to let me do things. Aunt Kitty was the only sibling who was not afraid to speak up to Mom and would always give her a good piece of her mind . . . she was a great confidant."

John became a very successful doctor. He later performed the first kidney transplant in the South, only the eighth in the country, on identical twins from Houma, Louisiana. Myra became closely associated with the Jazz scene in New Orleans. She and Dr. Edmund Suchon founded the New Orleans Jazz Club, and in 1950 she became the editor of the Club's publication, The Second Line, which was sent worldwide. In 1976, she was also instrumental in planning the memorial to Louis Armstrong ("Satchmo"), a bronze statue erected in Jackson Square. Satchmo was her favorite musician and friend, and she even named the family dog after this famous trumpet player. When he was playing in Germany, Satchmo sent her a Minolta camera because they both loved to take photographs. They also exchanged recipes. He sent her his favorite recipe for red beans and rice, a dish he loved that would also become the inspiration for his signature, "Red Beans and Ricely Yours."

Myra was often asked to be a guest columnist for the local States-Item newspaper writer, Tommy Griffin. Her writings were often clever and humorous. In Myra's early writings, she used the pen name of "Penny Whistle," a name representing the smallest musical instrument. Daughter Myra credits her own love of the visual and performing arts to her mother, who spent a lot of quality time cultivating this interest in her daughter. In a 1959 column, she had a vision of bringing a Jazz festival to New Orleans. They were successful in other cities and had never lost money for their investors. She was trying to drum up backers and is quoted as saying, "Unfortunately molasses slow New Orleans has made no effort in this direction . . . everyone is waiting for someone to sign the first check." Quint Davis took the lead, and in 1970, New Orleans had its first Jazz and Heritage Festival, which continues successfully to this day.

When Myra was fifty, she hired George Lewis' Jazz band to play for her birthday in the living room with immediate family as the only guests. The bass player leaned over to George. "When's all the peoples comin'?" She had so much fun that she saved her money and repeated this event ten years later for her sixtieth birthday with Clive Wilson's band. Again, only her husband and children were present. However, she did open all the windows for the neighbors' enjoyment.

Her life was Jazz. Black Musicians would often come to the house during the segregation years. John, who was more conservative, grew to accept the company of these musicians and respected Myra's work. Myra spent much time trying to get these men jobs at functions in a predominantly white society. Papa Celestine was a famous clarinet player whose band played locally for many years. When he died, Myra walked in his funeral along with hundreds of fans. It was then that she arranged in advance her own Jazz funeral with Archbishop Hannan. When Myra died of ovarian cancer on February 15, 1979, John and young Myra carried out her wishes. The eight-piece Jazz band, a hand-picked group of musicians, volunteered to play. They loved and respected Myra because she did so much for them. They played outside St. Francis of Assisi Church on State Street before and after the service. Later in the Lake Lawn Mausoleum near the crypt, the band played some of her favorites: "A Closer Walk With Thee," "Battle Hymn of the Republic," and "Down by the Riverside." There were no dry eyes. It was fitting that Myra, at the age of sixty-six, died as she lived, surrounded by family and having things her way.

Myra

And Then There Were Ten

Kathleen Cartan Loker Gibbons (Kitty)

Kathleen

Kathleen, known as Kitty and later Tima by her grandchildren, was the second of the six girls known as the "beautiful Loker girls." As a child, she was more homely than the rest. Although she hated exercise, she did skate and ride her bike until the age of eleven. Aunt Julia Walmsley, wife of Semmes Walmsley, tried to teach her to swim by throwing her into a swimming pool. This foolish act backfired because after that, she never went into another pool the rest of her life. If she had her way, she would rather play with little babies. In fact, she was proud of the fact that she changed diapers at the age of six. Mere probably took advantage of Kitty and asked her to do more than her fair share of helping out with the other siblings. However, Kitty felt comfortable in this role and would continue babysitting little children most of her life. She always offered to babysit her grandchildren, nieces, nephews, and great-grandchildren. She checked lessons, hemmed uniforms, polished school shoes, fixed favorite meals, and always stocked the fridge with all the special and favorite foods of those she was babysitting. Kathleen Van Horn said that she and husband Charlie invented places to go so Tima could babysit both nights.

Kitty was happiest around family. She worried about all of them. She became the confidant par excellence—you were able to talk to her about anything, and she never betrayed your trust. She sat in a chair with those long red fingernails, smoking one cigarette after another, usually wearing something pink, pink being her favorite color. She made you feel better after you had bared your soul, making you see the light and feel more at peace by the time you left her house. She was the one you could count on to relay family news. She was sincerely interested in everyone and loved them all the same. There has been no one to fill her shoes in family communication.

Kitty's great-granddaughter, Katie Van Horn, remembers how opinionated she was. "Any mention of nuns and she went off on a rant about how ridiculous it was that they did not wear habits anymore, and she was appalled to have seen the headmistress of Sacred Heart in shorts. But as opinionated as she was, she was also very thoughtful." When she did not approve of something, she would say, "It's perfectly outrageous." Tima fixed the foods they liked. Katie's brother, James, agrees that Tima indulged them with their favorite treats while they watched shows on TV like Picket Fences, Dr. Quinn, Medicine Woman, and Golden Girls. All three of them sat on the bed with the mattress sagging to one side, the side on which she sat for endless hours talking on the phone. Kitty kept Ghirardelli chocolate squares in the same drawer as her Alpine Menthol cigarettes. Katie added, "It was my job to run to the front room, get a new pack (which was often), and peel off the plastic wrapping. It probably wasn't the best example to be setting for a young child, but it was tradition." Semmes Favrot added that after the age of sixteen, he gave Tima a carton of cigarettes for both her birthday and Christmas. It was the perfect gift—practical and thoughtful.

As a child, Kathleen spent a lot of time in bed because the doctors had told Mere that they thought they saw a suspicious spot on her daughter's lung that, given the right conditions, might possibly develop into tuberculosis. The doctors were wrong, but Kathleen spent a lot of time in bed as a result of the diagnosis. After Holy Name grammar school, Kathleen attended the Academy of the Sacred Heart and later, Grand Coteau. Mere birthed all her babies at home, like so many people in those days. When Adele was to be born, Mere sent Babydoll and Kathleen to Grand Coteau, a Sacred Heart school in Sunset, Louisiana. The 1927 hurricane was approaching, and since the unpaved roads were bad and it was too difficult to return home, the nuns kept them at school the following year. Kitty spent most of her senior year in bed and did not graduate. She eventually got her strength back and returned home.

When it came time to make her debut, Kathleen put her foot down and refused. She was adamant that she "wasn't going to walk out in front of all those people," and she never really liked to dance—there was not much point to it as far as she was concerned. Kathleen was painfully shy, so she used sisters Janet and

Adele as an excuse to flirt with Jack Gibbons, who lived two doors away from the Lokers on Calhoun Street. She would run after her sisters, pretending to be scolding them, as a way to see Jack. Kitty did admit to smooching behind College Inn on Carrollton Avenue. Jack was outgoing, and he fell for this tall, slim, attractive gal. So, at age twenty, Kathleen married Jack on February 7, 1934. They had three children, Jack, Kay, and Cartan, and they lived with Mere and Pere during the early years of their marriage.

Kathleen had high standards and expected everyone to live up to them. No excuses were allowed. She loved her children very much but did not show much affection. She never had a lot of money, but she made sure that her children had everything they needed in order to do all the things that children and teenagers wanted to do. She was very proud of her family and knew exactly who she was. She never complained. Her daughter Kay writes, "I think her greatest gift to us was her giving us the same understanding and assurance that we could hold our heads up with pride anywhere. Money had nothing to do with it. It was that knowledge that allowed me to feel comfortable about where I came from and to concentrate on who I was and where I was going. It made my brothers and me better people. I will forever be grateful to my mother for that priceless gift."

Her husband Jack had a drinking problem, and the marriage eventually declined because of irreconcilable differences. After twenty-five years, Kathleen and Jack divorced. Kathleen spent a lot of time playing cards with Mere's sister, Carrie Irwin, and

Carrie's older friends. Kathleen hated lying and vulgarity, but she laughed when told risqué jokes that she heard at work or from her brothers. She was a strong woman and overcame some of her timidity by working at Dress Circle, a clothing store on St. Charles Avenue and later at Hampson House. She was great at her job and knew practically the entire city. Always well groomed, Kitty was never seen without her cultured pearls at work or at home. It is also said that she was never seen in a pair of pants.

Kathleen never liked talking about death, and in many ways, she was afraid to die. She had a burial plan that she prepaid for years. Since she wanted a proper burial without worrying her children, this independent woman made all the arrangements to carry out her wishes. In the end, she developed dementia, and when it got to the point where she could not live alone, her family put her in the Lambeth House. Kitty was perfectly miserable and would not come out of her room. Adele graciously offered for Kitty to come live with her. Thrilled with the idea, Kathleen moved into the front room of Adele's duplex.

It was incredibly sad to watch the physical and mental decline of the vibrant lady who took care of generations. Her independence and pride were chipped away piece by piece. But there is always humor in any story. Kitty started smoking when she and her husband Jack moved to Oklahoma, living on the army base. She was expected to entertain other officers and their wives. She was so nervous that someone offered her a cigarette to calm her down. It worked. Because Kitty had become a chain smoker long ago, the idea of Kitty smoking in Adele's home was a problem.

Two of Adele's grandchildren, who lived next to Adele in the other part of the duplex, visited often and were highly allergic to smoke. After a brief conference with God, Adele came up with a solution. When Kitty was down to her last cigarette, she demanded that Adele run out and get her a new pack. Adele simply said, "Kathleen, don't you remember what I told you? The doctors proved that cigarettes caused cancer and the tobacco companies had so many lawsuits against them, they went bankrupt. They no longer make any cigarettes." Shocked, Kitty said, "Oh, that's a damn shame." From that moment, she never pursued the smoking issue. When her grandchildren reminded her she used to smoke two packs a day, she denied every word.

Elated by this response, Adele tried her luck again. Kitty would sit in her chair in her pink bathrobe and watch TV until two or three in the morning. Naturally, the noise kept Adele awake. One night when Adele was ready to retire upstairs about eleven p.m., she turned off the TV. Kathleen yelped out, "Turn that back on . . . I was watching that." Adele gently turned toward her and said, "Oh, Kathleen, don't worry, the station is getting ready to go off the air and the station seal is about to come on the screen so there will not be any TV until tomorrow." Kathleen's response was, "Oh."

Kathleen lived with Adele for three years. The night Kitty died, December 20, 2004, Adele prayed over her on her final watch. At the service in Holy Name Church, everyone was asked to wear pink in honor of Kathleen aka Kitty and Tima. At the start of the service, all of her children, grandchildren, and great-grandchildren walked in unison down the church aisle to the front pews. And in the end, Kathleen never needed to worry about death—it was just a passing from one life to another—with the best pink send-off anyone at Holy Name had ever seen.

And Then There Were Ten

Margaret Carroll Loker (Babydoll)

Babydoll

It is said that "three's a charm," and so it was with the Loker girls. Third born Margaret Carroll Loker was often referred to as Peggy, but to her grandfather and older sister, she was "Babydoll." Her large brown twinkling eyes, Dresden skin, and two huge matching dimples delicately framing her mouth perfectly describe a babydoll. Older sister Myra climbed into Peggy's crib insisting that she was her personal "Babydoll." Mere came to the rescue, but the name stuck. The fact that there is an Aunt Babydoll in the Loker Family usually sends outsiders into gales of laughter, but to the family, it just makes everyone smile. Babydoll was born in 1914 and at the age of five months moved from St. Louis, Missouri, with her parents and two sisters to New Orleans. She spent first and second grade at Mrs. Miller's School, which was near Papoo's home. She then went to Miss Edith Aiken's School. During the seventh and eighth grades, Babydoll boarded at Grand Coteau, Louisiana. She was not wild about it because of all the rules, such as no eating between meals and no talking during meals. For goutée, the afternoon snack, the nuns served either a brownie on a saltine cracker or a banana or an orange with two pecans. During bath time, the nuns stayed in the bathroom to ensure there was no nudity. The girls had to wear their nightgowns out of the bathroom because they were never allowed to be seen nude. Babydoll explains, "So we were in there [the bathroom] a while until we learned to take off our gowns in the tub, and of course they would get wet. We quickly got in the tub for a quick bath and then had to maneuver the gown on again before we would leave the bath." Because the girls would flirt so much with the boys, there were no altar boys. The nuns and the students took care of the altar when they had daily mass.

"The town was little," Babydoll said, "maybe five families, including a hunchback family. Everyone in the family was hunchbacked. If our grades were decent, we were allowed to go in groups to visit this family. We thought it was exciting to get off school grounds." Fortunately, she had sister Kitty and cousin Augusta Walmsley to keep her company at Grand Coteau.

When Peggy was seventeen, her friend Virginia Harris (who was queen of Comus the year Babydoll was a page in the court) said that actor Cary Grant was coming to her house for dinner. If Babydoll came over, she could ride with them while Cary was taken to the train. Babydoll had no trouble making that decision. When she arrived at Virginia's house, she also met Bing Crosby's brother, Bob, who often came to New Orleans because his band played there at a nightclub called Club Forest. Babydoll used to flirt when Bob made the rounds in the room, visiting all the tables. One time at the club, he mentioned that he was putting on a skit for the show in which he needed some long red drawers. Trying to be helpful, Babydoll told Bob that she knew where to find a pair. She met him at the hotel where he was staying, and together they went to search for the drawers, first at D. H. Holmes, then Maison Blanche. Before long, they exhausted every potential store in the city, without success.

'After high school, Babydoll worked at Town and Country dress shop in New Orleans, but she was still expected to follow Loker house rules on dating: no dating until eighteen years of age, and the first year had to be double dates only. At parties, the girls carried dance cards. These were cards with sequential numbers imprinted on the cards for the number of each dance. The young ladies waited on one side of the room, young men on the other, after the boys had filled in the girls' dance cards.

While working at Town and Country in 1931, Babydoll was to have a date with a young navy man from Pensacola—a date she would end up breaking. In those days for entertainment, young people would go dancing at least four nights a week. On one of those days, her good friend Virginia Ligette needed a date for a gentleman who turned out to be Dave Cottrell. Babydoll giggles when she remembers that "he had me at those first four little words, 'Hi, how are you?' in that thick southern Mississippi accent."

Like her sister Myra, Babydoll modeled for Saks Fifth Avenue and traveled for Vogue magazine. She lived in New York for only one year and stayed mostly in the South after meeting Dave.

And Then There Were Ten

During this time, Dave, aspiring to be a lawyer, organized and played in the band called The Mississippians, which was the beginning of the Ole Miss band. Dave's musical talent originated in childhood where he specialized in the piano and the trumpet. By the time he got to college, he was so multitalented that he could play almost any instrument.

After dating for two years, Dave proposed to Peggy. The first time he asked her to marry him, she turned him down because she refused to raise children in the Methodist Church. Peyton shares, "The stress of the Depression makes steel out of iron. Like many family members, Babydoll emerged victorious from the challenge. The root of her character is in her love and understanding of her heritage and her genuine devotion and respect for her parents. This solid moral foundation allowed a Sacred Heart graduate to love and respect a north Mississippi Methodist. Peggy and Dad were true Christians, respecting each other's religions and sharing Christian values."

The second proposal of marriage issued included raising children Catholic. Babydoll accepted. At that time, the Catholic Church had strict rules about mixed marriages that do not exist today. Since Dave was methodist, they could not be married in the church, so the wedding ceremony took place at Mamee and Papoo's house on June 7, 1935, which happened to be Dave's birthday. Babydoll was twenty-three and Dave was thirty.

Early in their married life, which was before World War II, Dave and Babydoll, like many investors at the time, began buying properties for investment purposes. After Dave purchased four properties in Mississippi, the bank told him that they thought he had bought enough. A West Point graduate with a photographic memory, Dave wanted to give himself to his country during World War II, but he was leery because of his age as he was already in his early thirties. He went to Washington, D.C., to ask the advice of his friend Senator Harrison, who suggested that Dave volunteer for his country. Having four years in military school, Dave enlisted as a captain in the army the day after Dave III was born. He was stationed in Pine Bluff, Arkansas, where the army was working on chemical warfare.

After four and a half years living in Pine Bluff, Dave took his family back to Gulfport, Mississippi. They temporarily lived at the Edgewater Hotel where large buffet meals including crab and shrimp cocktails, vegetables, meats, and desserts could be purchased for $1.25. The family ultimately moved to Bert Avenue in Gulfport, where they lived for more than fifty years. In 1996, Dave died at the age of eighty-six. Not wanting their mother to live alone, the boys moved Peggy to Houston where she would be close to them. After selling many of those wonderful antiques and taking others with her, Babydoll moved to Houston, Texas, to be with her boys. She could be reached day or night for a chat. Since she dozed on and off during the day, she would stay up most of the night, often talking to baby sister Adele in the wee hours of the morning. They often talked about how the Cottrell's house on Bert Avenue was destroyed by Hurricane Katrina on August 29, 2005.

Before Dave III was born, Babydoll lost an infant, Margaret Carroll Loker Cottrell, whose stomach was not fully closed. In 1945, second son Peyton was born. Babydoll stayed busy as a mother. Living on the Gulf Coast, the children were immersed in all water activities, especially fishing. When the days of sending the boys, between the ages of nine and eleven, upstairs for after lunch, naps in the summer were over, the boys eventually started fishing offshore. When they were a day or two late returning, Peggy would think nothing of sending Dave directly from his law office in his suit and hat out in the Gulf to find one of the boys, usually David. Then she would alert the coast guard to send a search and rescue boat. David said the guard knew her by her first name because she called them quite frequently.

One of Babydoll's favorite pastimes was her weekly bridge game, playing with three tables. Twelve women would arrive for three hours' worth of telling jokes, sharing local gossip, and enjoying tasty lunches. Babydoll was a great cook and a marvelous storyteller, and she would keep everyone in stitches with gales of laughter. David confirms that not only was the loudest laughter hers, but she also had an upbeat, positive, and happy personality. She was rarely seen in bad spirits.

Another of Peggy's hobbies was antique collecting. She and best friend Vivian Hewes would jump in the car and drive to Mobile, Alabama, or north Mississippi for serious antique shopping while Dave was offshore fishing. While Dave brought home fish, many of Peggy's purchases would not appear until some occasion later in the year. When she was not antiquing, she loved to come to New Orleans to visit her family. She would get together with her mother, siblings, nieces, and nephews. Visits with the girls, including Mere's sister, Carrie, were usually spent wiping away tears of laughter. Babydoll's laughter usually drowned out sister Kitty's giggles. Any of the younger generation considered it a privilege to be included in the mix. It was not only fun but also a wonderful way to understand family history and politics.

Peggy's loyalty to New Orleans reached beyond family—she was a devoted fan of Tulane and LSU. Peyton shares the following story:

In 1958, Mother, Dad, David, and I attended an Ole Miss/LSU game at Tiger Stadium. Dad had been president of the Ole Miss Alumni Association in 1949 and currently sat on the Board of Trustees of the Schools of Higher Learning of Mississippi. His old friend, Governor White, had appointed him to the board in 1954. The governor, Senator John Stennis, the entire school board, and other Mississippi dignitaries shared the two adjoining box seats right on the 50-yard line at Tiger Stadium. We had all enjoyed the Ole Miss Fight song, the Ole Miss cheerleaders, the band, and pre-game festivities. I was seated on Mother's right hand side and David was on her left. The game started, the highly charged fans screamed battle cries, and the teams fiercely struggled to score. The game was close. Later, Ole Miss kicked off. The ball was soundly kicked into the LSU end zone. Billy Cannon caught the ball and proceeded to run down the Ole Miss sideline. The LSU stands were going crazy. The sound was deafening but not as loud as the silence on the Ole Miss side. Only a few gasps and low murmurings were heard except, of course, from Mother. As Billy ran by, Mother rose out of her Ole Miss 50-yard line box seat and yelled, "GO, BILLY, GO!!!" David and I were embarrassed and attempted to restrain Mother. We grabbed her arms, one son on each side. She didn't even acknowledge our efforts as she continued to scream "GO, BILLY, GO!!!" Mother did not even attend LSU or Tulane. Her loyalty to her family was symbolized by her affection for those schools. The ride back to Gulfport was long and quiet.

Peggy was blessed with children, grandchildren, and daughters-in-law who loved her and were proud of her. She was a remarkable lady of virtue who not only remained steadfast in her beliefs but also positive and happy. When people called her on the telephone, they could almost "see" her smile because she was always delighted to hear from everyone, a characteristic she had embodied her whole life. Babydoll died in Houston, Texas, on May 14, 2014.

Babydoll

And Then There Were Ten

David Cartan Loker, Jr. ("Dave," Brother)

Dave

Pere must have been elated April 27, 1916, to finally have a son after three daughters. Dave, affectionately referred to as Brother by the family, was named for his father. He was born in Papoo's house at 2507 Prytania Street, a compound that, with all the gardens, took up a quarter of the block. With church being next to the house and school only a block away, there was little need to leave the compound during those early years. Three more siblings followed before Mere and Pere moved to Calhoun Street.

For a very brief period in the eighth grade, Dave entertained the idea of entering the priesthood. Although this notion was short-lived, he got up one day in Holy Name Church, walked right up to the altar, climbed up into the pulpit, and read the gospel. The priest did nothing, and after the gospel was finished, Dave walked back to his seat. Nothing was ever said, and that was the closest he ever got to the priesthood.

Howard Black, Pere's adopted son, roomed with Dave. These were two good-looking fellas who got along beautifully. After Holy Name School, both entered Jesuit High School.

Dave was exceedingly handsome . . . dark hair, blue eyes, and physically strong and fit. Although he had lots of girlfriends, they did not interfere with his athletic career. Playing ball in the street prepared him to throw the discus at Jesuit, where he also played football. In 1933, Dave was the star punter for Jesuit's championship team. He used the famous "drop kick" play, which was engineered ten years earlier by football star Johnny Menville (who would later become Dave's brother-in-law). Dave's enormous success in athletics brought him scholarship offers from Tulane, LSU, Oklahoma, Tennessee, Michigan, and Notre Dame. Neither one of his parents attended any of his games nor encouraged him to pursue the scholarships. His daughters agree that his life might have been so different if he had had some parental direction emphasizing the importance of education. Dave was very aware of the family's need for money, so the day after graduation at Jesuit, instead of preparing for college, he worked at the Standard Oil Company station at the corners of Louisiana Avenue and St. Charles Avenue to help earn income for the family.

Dave was introverted, romantic, and sensitive. The girls flocked around him. Insecure about his place in life, he sometimes appeared arrogant. His daughter, Leslie, wrote,

> I think his lack of self-esteem and confidence left him rudderless, without any defining direction in which to go. How

fearful he must have felt so much of his life. However, he covered his fear and lack of direction with a certain false bravado. He quit one job after another, obtained through Walmsley connections [insurance, banking and stock brokering]; ironically the reason he gave for leaving these positions, he said, was that his employer[s] wanted to take advantage of his "social connections" to bring in business. He was proud of his mother's heritage [Leslie said he never mentioned his father's family to me] and in the next breath, he disdained it. I think he did this out of fear that he was not worthy and could never live up to those illustrious ancestors' accomplishments. He felt great guilt for his failures and took little pride in his successes. He was a man with enormous inner conflict which resulted in severe bouts of depression throughout his adult life.

During high school, Dave met Sheelah Rafferty while she was attending McGehee's School. Like many New Orleanians, they would spend weekends in Pass Christian, Mississippi, where her family lived. She went to college for two years. Then, at age nineteen, she and Dave, twenty-five, decided that they were madly in love and wanted to be married. Brother was blissfully happy, but he could not provide for his family. After six years, Sheelah moved their daughters, Leslie and Sharon, to the Pass so that Brother would have no responsibilities except to get his life in order. The understanding was that if he could keep a job and pay off his debts, the family would move back to New Orleans to be together again. Unfortunately, this was not the case and in 1950, when Leslie was six and Sharon was four, Sheelah filed for divorce. Dave was heartbroken and could not get over the fact that Sheelah left him. He loved her until the day he died. He withdrew temporarily from his children, moving in with Mere, probably due to depression. After three years apart from Leslie and Sharon, he reentered their lives with great determination.

In the mid-1950s, Dave met Hazel Weeks, a wealthy widow from Birmingham, who owned a Jax Brewery distributorship in Baton Rouge. She had two young children, Barbara Ann and Driscoll. At this time, Dave was running a concession stand at a bowling alley in Baton Rouge. The couple married, and Dave took over the distributorship. With little training, he lost it after three years. They then moved to Orange, Texas, where Dave worked at another bowling alley. Hazel was an honest, hardworking woman who sold furniture and worked her way up to manager. She loved Dave and married him in good faith. He, on the other hand, was never in love with her. It was during this time that Dave consistently visited both his daughters and took them for Christmas and summer vacations. He went to school graduations and wrote regularly to both. He made a great effort to stay in their lives. After fourteen years, Dave left Hazel and moved to Poplarville, Mississippi. He was never officially divorced, however, and Hazel died shortly after he left her.

When Dave's granddaughter, Lilah, was born, he bonded with this beautiful wispy blonde little girl. At that time, Sharon and her husband, Trailer, were living in New Orleans with their daughter. Brother would come in from Poplarville every Sunday to take Lilah to see Mere and visit the park and the zoo. What he missed doing as a father, he religiously made up as a grandfather. When Sharon moved to Ocean Springs, Mississippi, and Collin was born, Brother made the trek to Ocean Springs to visit his grandchildren. When he was in the bowling business, many of his nieces and nephews would spend time with him, honing their bowling skills. He was often seen smoking a cigar and calling everyone "child." Conversations with him would always end up being philosophical.

When Brother moved to Poplarville, a small town with few resources, Sharon said he felt an overwhelming need to atone for his sins. He spent the rest of his life helping and rescuing others in need. Adele referred to him as "St. Francis of Assisi" because he would help anyone who was down and out. Leslie refers to him as "a one-man social service agency for the poor, the abused, the needy, and the forgotten. He gathered clothes and money for them, tutored them in reading, helped fill out bureaucratic forms and, in a pinch, took some of them into his home." He once helped a young girl get a tuition waiver for college, and he started the Poplarville Toys for Tots program, which was taken over after his death by the local police and fire departments.

Dave died in 1977 of skin cancer that had metastasized. His son-in-law, Trailer, a master craftsman and artist, made and carved his casket. At the funeral, the mayor applauded Dave's many contributions. There were spontaneous testimonials by the town's residents enumerating "Mr. Dave's" kindnesses throughout the years. In the end, Dave spent his life making a positive difference in other people's lives. He had found his place, and it was a testimony that made his family proud.

Miriam Walmsley Loker Ogden ("Mimi," Sister)

Mimi

In 1919, Miriam Walmsley Loker, the fifth Loker to be born on Prytania Street, was named for Mere's sister who had died of pneumonia. Miriam's name was shortened to Mimi and, alternately, to Sister by the family. Since Mamee could not bear to hear a child named "Miriam," Miriam's name was changed to "Sister" to appease Mamee. They already had "Brother" and now had a counterpart. Sister was a sweet girl whose best friend was Sylvia Harry—they were inseparable. Timid in junior high, Sister only started dating her senior year at Holy Name, breaking the "eighteen-year" dating rule.

Mimi made her debut at the age of nineteen, and she was the belle of the ball. At that time, she wore her beautiful long chestnut hair wound in braids around her head. When she was a maid in the Rex Court on Mardi Gras day, actor Errol Flynn asked her out on a date. She did not go, but what a thrill for such a young girl! During that debut year, she received four proposals of marriage.

The one she accepted was that of Dr. Henry Ogden, who was thirteen years her senior. They were married October 16, 1939.

Mimi lived in a three-bedroom house at 258 Pine Street, in which six children were born in ten years. Miriam, Zizi, and Lucille arrived in the first four years, with a small break before Chip, Barry, and Peter followed. She had to go to bed for the last three pregnancies, each costing her $1,000 in prenatal care before they were born. In those days, mothers stayed home and raised the children, often using a raised eyebrow to keep everyone in check. Mimi had it covered with three mirrors strategically hung so that she could inspect the situation from any vantage point. Another trick of the trade was to tell children that Mom had eyes in the back of her head. This deception was perpetuated by all the Loker girls, and when all the stops were pulled, out came the metal and wooden shoe horns, which Mimi used judiciously. Once, however, Chip came running down the stairs, jumped onto the beautiful dining room table, and split it in two. Mimi was so angry she walked around the block three times before dealing with Chip. By the time she returned, she was calmer, but Chip also got the dreaded shoehorn.

Mimi was determined to teach her children morals, manners, values, and virtues. She made them see that it was important to be self-made and not merely to rely on the laurels of ancestors. She had a good sense of humor and was fun to be around. She not only made sure that everyone had a costume for Mardi Gras and Halloween, but she herself joined in the fun. She would think nothing of going to a party with a lampshade on her head, blackening her teeth, or wearing a horrible wig. One Mardi Gras,

Lucille remembered her mother's costume was hilarious. This particular time, she wore a tacky dress. "She sewed a pocket in the bosom of her dress in which she was able to pull out hot dogs through the dress. When she sat down, she would pull up her skirt, and you could see a slip made out of the Sunday funny papers. So she would sit down reading the comics while eating the hot dogs."

Zizi tells the story about Mimi painstakingly applying ghost-vampire makeup for Halloween. "After she donned a to-the-floor, hooded, black velvet cape and held a candle to her face, she slowly walked down the driveway. When I saw her, I thought I would expire on the spot. I was petrified. I ran through our backyard, jumped the fence, and landed in the empty lot next door. It was my mother. And I knew it. And I watched her put the costume on!" As outlandish as Mimi could be, she also sewed beautiful Easter dresses every year for her girls. She had exquisite taste—natural, graceful, and refined. She also loved to entertain. In addition to the many family parties, she often hosted medical parties. At this one particular party, New Orleans Mayor Chep Morrison brought Argentina's Eva Perrone, who later became a patient of Henry's.

One of the highlights of the year was Christmas night at Sister's. After cooking an enormous Christmas dinner for her family, she would have all of her siblings and their children over to the house for Christmas cheer, including presents for all the children. All the nieces and nephews unanimously agree that it was this very occasion every year that they all fondly remember. It was one of the few times the entire family gathered, other than weddings and funerals. It is clearly the reason most of the first cousins are close.

Sister was a good listener and gave advice when needed. All the girls concur that Sister would wait up and listen to her daughters' stories after they came home from their dates. Mimi had the gift of gab and could talk on any topic—from politics to religion. She would make time for everyone, including all family members. Jay Menville frequently dropped by the house for a visit—he loved her and confided in her. Barry said she had a talent for making a person feel like they were the most important person in Sister's life. He also said Sister loved him the most.

Summers were spent going on vacations to Florida or renting a home in Pass Christian, Mississippi. Later, television changed some of the family dynamics. In 1952, Henry and Mimi bought a fourteen-bedroom house at 2124 Palmer Avenue, which included a secret passageway that wrapped all around the upstairs of the house. Miriam explained that the house had been the caretaker's residence for the Audubon Plantation, and the servants used the secret passageways to get to the bedrooms.

Henry thought it was healthy to eat liver. So once a month, Erline, the maid, would serve the liver to the children while the parents ate later. Miriam recounted, "Because we would hear about the poor starving children somewhere, we would have to eat everything on our plate. Hating the liver, we would throw it behind the large china sideboard. Mother was always calling the Orkin man to spray again because of the roaches in the dining room! It wasn't until they sold the house when I was twenty-six and the sideboard was moved that I saw the liver was still there. I fessed up about the liver escapades but fortunately she did not care because she was busy with the move."

Henry Ogden had planned to be a surgeon, but a golf cart accidentally ran over his hand, so he decided to go back to medical school. He switched his specialty to neurology and allergy, concentrating on the specialty of headaches. He published Your Headache and was asked to be on the Today Show to promote his book. He also invented Fiornal and helped to invent Librium and Nivea cream. He loved his wife, Mimi, but he had a drinking problem and the marriage suffered. He would defer to Mimi for everything from medical issues to discipline. Barry laments that "Dad did not pay much attention to us growing up. Mimi had a terrible time for years because she did not want to divorce our father until we were old enough to understand." After she divorced him, Henry died the next August of 1968 at the age of sixty-two.

After Mimi divorced Henry, she met Jim Monteith, who was the opposite of Henry. Mimi and Jim shared many common interests, including running a small antique store on Oak Street. They lived happily on Green Street for several years. In 1980, they sold the house and moved to Poplarville, where Mimi became active in many charitable organizations. She had the brilliant idea to start the Blueberry Jubilee as a means of raising money for the local hospital. The Good Morning America television show interviewed her via telephone about the fundraiser. The

Jubilee, using many of her own recipes, was highly successful and is still held annually today. Sister is famous for starting the Blueberry Jubilee, and her name is the answer to one of the Mississippi trivia game questions.

In 1988, Mimi developed Parkinson's disease, a disease that left her totally debilitated. Daughter Miriam noted that in the last three years of Sister's life, Sister lost everything in which she excelled. She would spend two hours getting dressed and had to use a microphone to be heard. In 1991, the doctor discovered she had lung cancer and gave her three months to live. Her daughter Miriam quit her job and moved into Mimi's house to take care of her because this time, Jim had failing health himself and was physically unable to take care of his wife. With prayer and the grace of the Holy Spirit, Miriam helped her mother conquer her fear of dying. They had many witty, wonderful conversations that prepared Mimi so that when the time came, she was ready "to go home." Sister died May 9, 1991.

Mimi

And Then There Were Ten

George Hannibal Loker

George

"Blessed are the peacemakers for they shall inherit the earth." Peacemakers are usually patient, good listeners, and negotiators—George Hannibal Loker was all these things. A middle child, the second male, George was the epitome of a Southern gentleman. He never gave his parents any trouble, got along with his siblings, did well in school, and was an all-around good guy, which allowed him to slip through the cracks. There were no wild stories, no raucous parties or extreme sports fanaticism about George; in fact, there was not one negative thing said about him during his life. What became clearly evident was that he had an impeccable character.

When George was not at Holy Name School, he was fishing in the park or playing ball with his brothers. Later, he advanced to football and baseball in Fortier High School. He joined the baseball Junior Varsity at Fortier and was considered to be good enough to play professional baseball, but when the Depression came, George felt the responsibility to his family and he went to work, like so many other boys. He was quiet, handsome, and a good dancer. Even his stuttering did not handicap George with the girls. They were crazy about him. He respected women and treated them well.

George made all three of the family moves on Calhoun Street: 1456, 1722, and 1915. When he was living at 1915 Calhoun, he fell off of the second story back porch. The backside of his thigh hit the water faucet, but he never complained. It was just not his nature. Once he was in Audubon Park with Tom and Walmsley, eating peanut butter from a knife. He cut his tongue and it began to bleed profusely. Stoically, he did not complain—he knew he had done a foolish thing.

In high school, George and his friend Leland Montgomery were in charge of a "script dance" in the old Audubon Tea Room in the park. A script dance is a "pay as you go" type of dance; each person pays an admission fee (cover charge) in the amount that will cover refreshments, the band, and the rental of the hall. George and Leland were responsible for collecting the money. One boy decided to come in without paying the entrance fee. George approached him and said, "I know you think I'm easy because I look easy, but let's take this outside." Leland said George took that guy outside and "beat the hell out of him," shocking everyone.

Son Beau tells how George did not have the temperament to be the vice president of a company. However, he and his siblings never questioned George's feelings for his wife, Elsie. "He defended her whenever I would spout off, much to my irritation.

I wanted a kindred spirit, not someone telling me I was wrong. But that was Dad—always trying to make me see both sides when I just wanted support for my stupid (in retrospect) reasoning."

George may not have been gregarious, but he had good leadership qualities. He was grand master (president) of TKS (high school fraternity). In World War II, he volunteered for his country, not waiting for the draft, and enlisted in the army. When he was stationed in Scotland as a private, he met the queen of England twice and ended up singing a duet with her, "You Are My Sunshine." In a very short time, his stuttering disappeared and he was promoted to the rank of corporal. He served in the Battle of the Bulge and was also under General George C. Patton's command. As an army engineer, he spent a good part of his duty building bridges.

After the war, he got a job with King Candy Company. It was then that baby sister Adele introduced him to Elsie Vantreight, who at that time was living at Fannie Burke's Boarding House on Prytania Street and working for Travelers' Aid. They fell madly in love, and within five months, they were married in her hometown, Victoria, British Columbia, Canada. Although she was Episcopalian, they were married in St. Andrew's Catholic Church on April 21, 1951, with the reception at the beautiful family home situated on an acre of land. Tom was best man and the only Loker relative to attend the wedding. They honeymooned in Niagara Falls.

George changed jobs to work for the Whitman Candy Company. While he traveled, he wrote love letters to his wife Elsie—peacemakers are romantics too! Eventually, the children arrived: Helen,

Beau, Caroline, and Martha. With six in the family and Elsie working and going to school, George made a career change and started working for and eventually managing several bowling alleys. First at Mid-City Lanes (now Rock-n-Bowl), then Pelican Lanes, followed by Orbit Lanes, and eventually Mardi Gras Lanes. Helen said, "My dad wasn't always a great provider for his family, but he did try."

George was always slow moving, and nothing would make him go any faster, to the frustration of all around him. However, this patient man put his family first and found time to be available and to consistently play with his children. It was nothing to see George in the blow-up kiddie pool—Elsie used to say it was like having five kids around the house. Beau never saw that as a problem since none of the other dads in the neighborhood were as involved. George taught Beau how to ride his bike and to talk like Donald Duck. If he wasn't taking the kids to the park or drawing Mickey Mouse on their hands, attending basketball games and tournaments, he was encouraging people in their endeavors to get through a difficult task or a challenging time. At Mardi Gras, George would exchange his usual bowtie (his supply exceeded fifty) for a red nightshirt with the red night cap that he used for a costume, year after year.

Beau shares a story from his adolescence.

> As a teenager, I didn't drink—at all. I did, however, stay out late and run around to different friends' houses without the parents knowing where we were—obviously all before cell phones. So, I was getting in very early one Sunday morning as Dad was rising. He asked me where I had been and

I told him I had been at someone's house but had fallen asleep. He said "Balderdash" (kinda) and asked me where I had really been. I sheepishly told him and he only told me to go up and get some sleep. When I woke up later, my mother asked me where I had been. Reasoning that it hadn't worked on ole Dad, I told her the truth. She looked at me with a puzzled, then irritated look on her face and said, "Your father told me you had been at a friend's house and had fallen asleep." Sheesh! Dad was covering for me and I went and got him in trouble. We laughed about that incident later on, in the eighties.

George was there for more than just his family. Whenever anyone needed anything, George would be called. He would drop what he was doing to help them out—friends, family, and neighbors alike. With the help of do-it-yourself books, he became proficient at fixing things from plumbing to electrical to carpentry, and even some car repairs. The neighborhood kids referred to him as "Uncle George," an uncle everyone wanted but very few had. He was even-keeled—he rarely got mad, but when he did, he simply would clench his fist and refer to the scoundrel as a jerk or a jackass.

George adored all his children, so when the grandchildren started arriving, he would approach both of his daughters, who lived in New Orleans, and volunteer to babysit. Helen admitted that she only had to pay a babysitter twice because her parents loved to babysit. George would allow the young grandgirls to put stickers and ribbons in his hair or bury him up to his neck in the sand. He was as great a grandfather as he was a dad.

George took Jesuit's motto, "A man for others," to heart. Faithful to the Adoration Chapel, he would also count and deposit Sunday mass collections for Holy Name Church. He was awarded the St. Louis medal for his work at Holy Name.

George was also interested in fighting crime in New Orleans. He initiated the "Crimestoppers" organization and was responsible for starting the Neighborhood Watch groups in several neighborhoods. He would dress up as McGruff, the Crimestoppers' mascot, at parades, parties, and school fairs to promote the police work.

Caroline adds,
> He was also a charter member of the C.O.P.S. II (Citizens On Patrol S***), another community sponsored support group for the Second District of the NOPD. Several other NOPD Districts copied the Second District successes. Dad used to do a lot of the legwork and behind the scenes work and never really looked for the glory and praise for his efforts. He solicited donations from various businesses and, over a period of about fifteen years or so, he raised very close to $1 million dedicated solely for the Second District—for horses to patrol the district, for bullet proof vests for the officers, for scooters and various training for the men and women, for rewards and awards for the officers and for the annual Mardi Gras breakfasts during the Mardi Gras season. The Roll Call Room in the Second District police station is named the "George Loker Roll Call Room" in his memory.

In 1992, the Chamber of Commerce awarded him the "Crime Abatement Tribute" for his selfless commitment to improving the quality of life and opportunity in our community.

George's allegiance to people did not stop with the community. He was equally devoted to his siblings—all one had to do was call and he would drop what he was doing. When Adele's husband, Bill Hughs, died, George voluntarily stepped into the role of more than just an uncle. Since he only lived two doors down the street from Adele, George was there every single day, playing with the children, helping with their homework, and later fatherly duties of escorting the girls to various functions—always with a smile.

In the early 1990s, George had been diagnosed with Parkinson's Disease, and in April 1997, Elsie was diagnosed with this same cruel disease. In June 1997, he told Caroline, "Your mother is still as beautiful as the first day I met her and I love her more now than I did way back when!" Elsie was a difficult but very hard-working woman who helped and financially supported both sides of her family, all the while raising four children of her own without any family support. George only saw the good in her, as he did in everyone.

Four months after Elsie's diagnosis, George asked to go to the hospital. While waiting to go there, he simply stopped breathing. He died as he lived—quietly, not wanting to make trouble for anyone, always putting others first. This kind and gentle peacemaker had finally made his last peace. George died August 14, 1997.

And Then There Were Ten

Sylvester Pierce Walmsley Loker (Wam)

Walmsley

Walmsley, or Wam for short and named for Uncle P. (Sylester Pierce Walmsley), was born April 5, 1923. The seventh child and third boy, he arrived between George and Tom. Like the rest of the Lokers, Walmsley attended Holy Name School, then Jesuit, and Fortier High Schools. He was tall, handsome, and a wonderful athlete who followed Tom in every athletic pursuit. Both were experts in pass snatching, blocking, and tackling, and were top-notch ends for the Prep League in 1941. Tom defended for the Blue Jays and Wam the Tarpons. In a crushing blow to Fortier (Jesuit 46—Fortier 6), Walmsley told the Times-Picayune, "Tom and I played against each other. I played fullback and end. Both of us had the same number . . . 36. One of my kicks was blocked and Tom received it. He was the best punter in the state with an average of 45 yards; my average was 41 yards." Walmsley had started a Jesuit but left because he was accused of doing something he did not do—carving on a desk. A righteous man, he transferred to Fortier, which at that time was a top-ranked school. Because of his skill at football, Walmsley was given a scholarship to Tulane University where he was an amateur boxer and Green Wave Football Team member. Jack Gibbons tells the story that Wam was temporarily kicked off the team by Coach Monk Simmons before the infamous Tulane/LSU game because he came to a practice drunk. Wam, unable to defend himself, later admitted that it was the first time he got caught. But without money for tuition, he was only able to attend Tulane his freshman year.

Walmsley had a severe hearing problem that had existed since college; it was constantly draining. Because of this, the U.S. government labeled him 4F—unable to serve in the military. Walmsley was absolutely devastated. He applied to every branch of the service, including the merchant marines, without success. He grew bitter, angry, and began getting into fist fights with servicemen to prove himself. He claimed to hold the record for downing a sixteen-ounce beer in seven or eight seconds, and people began calling him "Wildman," a name that followed for a long time. He eventually got over his frustration at being 4F, yet as tough as he was on the outside, he was a kind, gentle, loving soul who would never hurt a flea. In the summer of 1951, Wam turned twenty-nine and married Carrol Reagan. Together they had Buzz, David, and Cindy. Their marriage was short-lived because after six years, Carrol left with the children and moved out of state. Thereafter, the children's memories of Wam were largely based on summer vacations spent with him.

Walmsley was outgoing—he never met a stranger. This talent helped him in sales, but he hated being cooped up in an office.

After he left the insurance business, he worked in a gas station so he could be outdoors. Later he got into automobile sales.

Walmsley was a guy's guy, yet a sweetheart and gentleman with the women. He would take the kids to play pool at Uncle Dave's pool hall, then take them fishing. He liked the sport of fishing and not just eating his catch. What he did enjoy was peanut butter, eating a jar a day while he was growing up. It became a staple in his adult life. He told Buzz that peanut butter would help him keep his hair. Wam spread peanut butter on just about anything—tomato sandwiches, P.B. and tuna, or whatever was around. This was his version of cooking.

Besides playing cards and pool, Walmsley was an avid bowler, winning many trophies, and he taught all of his children and nephews the art of the game. He was a sports fanatic—later watching Saints games, taking up golf, and even playing in the Senior Olympics, winning medals in both basketball and discus.

Athletics were not the only thing that occupied Walmsley's time. He was a good dancer, a creative one, having the gene that probably goes back to Isadora Duncan, Pere's second cousin. He would do the dance called the "N****r Shuffle" in which he would move his feet and swing his hips, gyrating and undulating to the rhythm of the music and drawing a crowd. The more he got into the movements, the more the crowd would beg for more. The shuffle was definitely his signature dance!

After seven years as a single man, Wam married Norma Jackson in 1964. They lived in Houma, Louisiana, and remained married until Walmsley's death in 1990. All their offspring agree that it was a special version of the Brady Bunch—yours, mine, and ours. Buzz, David, and Cindy from the first marriage, Buster and Kim from the second, and three from Norma's previous marriage. Walmsley maintained devotion and loyalty to his children, mother, and his brothers and sisters his whole life. He would bring his children to see Mere on Sundays as often as he could. He adored his children, and all of them knew it. He was never afraid to show his feelings and never hesitated to say, "I love ya" and give great big "bear crushing hugs" to the boys. "Even an injury did not prevent him from being there for us." Buster writes that he would sit in the bleachers, holding onto his crutches (recently breaking a leg that had been in a cast), watching and cheering at his son's football game. "He was proud of all his kids. He was there whenever I needed him, even the times when my wild side got the best of me. Daddy wasn't perfect, and neither am I, but he taught me to deal with it and never give up."

Wam was not the one to go to the doctor, but in June of 1990, he went in for exploratory surgery, thinking the doctor was going to remove his gallbladder. When they opened him up and saw widespread stomach cancer, the doctors gave him three months to live. Kim and Buster did a wonderful job of taking care of their father. Adele offered to take care of him in September, and he was in her home close to two months before he died, almost three months to the day from his diagnosis.

Walmsley was a good man—a great big teddy bear who loved life and lived it to the fullest. He loved everyone, and they knew it. He died September 12, 1990.

And Then There Were Ten

Thomas Jenkins Semmes Loker

Tom

Eighth in the Loker clan was Thomas Jenkins Semmes Loker, born March 19, 1924. Like the rest of the family, Tom attended Holy Name School, but he was the most mischievous. When he was in second or third grade, he decided he did not want to go to school, so he hid under Mere's house on Calhoun Street. Eventually, the school called Mere to report his absence and inquire if he was sick. Panicked, she searched everywhere and even called her mother, Mamee, to join the search. By the afternoon, the police had been contacted, but Tom was nowhere to be found. Finally, weary of the dark, he decided to make a clean break from his retreat and greeted Mere. Mere was so relieved to see him that he escaped the spanking he might have deserved. He got up bright and early the next day, and nothing more was said.

Tom was adorable and had beautiful curly black ringlets. When he was a child, people would stop him on the street and ask who he was. He got along well with his three older brothers. There was never any rivalry and very little fighting because they seemed to have fun with everything including once during a flood, when Tom and Walmsley carried people in a rowboat across St. Charles Avenue.

Like his brothers, Tom was a tremendous athlete, and when he got to Jesuit, he was linked to his brother Dave, labeled "Loker with the Educated Toe" because of how far he could kick a football. He once kicked a ball from the Tulane football field and broke a third-floor classroom window on Tulane's campus. An accomplished kicker and wide receiver, Tom lettered and was all-state in football at Jesuit. He was a champion discus thrower and competed in basketball and track.

One night, Tom came in tight (tipsy, drunk). Pere smelled beer on his breath, so the next night Pere bought some beer and invited Tom to drink one. Tom finished the bottle and Pere offered him a second. Hedging, Tom reluctantly drank the second and proceeded to get very sick. Ironically, Tom later became the distributor for two breweries but always held his beer.

Two months prior to his graduation from Jesuit, he was drafted at the age of 18. Tom joined the Marine Corps, 4th Division. As a part of his tour of duty, he was sent to Tinian, Iwo Jima, and Saipan where he saw the horrors of war through personal combat. He was discharged after World War II was over. After he returned, he did not speak about any of his experiences, like so many veterans. It was five years before he could speak about the war because everyone in his battalion was killed. He was the sole survivor. He returned home to attend Tulane University for a short time and played football for the Green Wave as a kicker. His daughter Peggy writes, "The New York Giants had taken notice of his kicking ability and were interested in drafting him to play professional football. Nothing became of this because after two years at Tulane, he quit school to work full time after his father died."

Tom was six foot four, good-looking, and funny, and he could tell one joke after another and keep people laughing for hours. He was a natural born clown. One day, Tom told Adele, who was very gullible, that Sr. Stephens, affectionately called SteamBoat, loved him so much that she kept him in the seventh grade for three years. Tom loved watching Adele's face. Whenever he saw the nieces and nephews, his stock greeting was, "I'm so glad you got to see me today!"

Tom did more than tell jokes. He liked to dance and was a wonderful jitterbugger. He had lots of acquaintances and many girlfriends, and he met Betty June Bujol while both were working at the Jax Brewery Company in 1956. Four years later, they were married at the St. Louis Cathedral with the reception at Henry and Mimi Ogden's home on Palmer Avenue. Tom was a strong, devoted, honest, hardworking, and God-fearing man who adored his family and children. Tom and Betty had three children—Elizabeth Anne (Beth), Margaret (Peggy) Carroll, and Thomas Jenkins Semmes Loker, Jr. (Tommy). After Tom married in 1959, Betty never worked another day in her life and never did without anything. They were not rich, but she and her children were provided for during their twenty-eight years of marriage before Tom's death.

Tom also had a sense of community and putting others first. He rarely took a vacation (he was afraid of flying). He was always sending Betty and her sister, Mootsie, on cruises and vacations together with the children. He would solicit business for food and non-perishable donations in return for playing Santa Claus at no charge. In return, he would give these donations to the church for the less fortunate who had nothing for Christmas. Although some people made fun of him in the Santa suit he wore to work, it did not matter to him. It was a small price to pay for all the good he was doing for others. After fourteen years of living in Algiers, Louisiana, Tom was offered a job with Falstaff Brewery Company based in Jackson, Mississippi, so he moved his family there. When Falstaff closed in 1978, he was offered a job as a manager of Jim Carey Distributing Company in LaPlace, Louisiana, and worked there until his death nine years later.

Tom's primary concern was providing for his family. Tommy remembers, "When he was sick with cancer, he went to work the day before he was put in the hospital for a procedure that never happened. His health went down quickly and the doctor was never able to perform the operation. I knew that he was not feeling well but he had to work because that is what he needed to do."

Tom's work ethic and character were exemplified in the life he led, a life he devoted to other people. Under all the smoke and mirrors of laughter and joking, Tom was a man of principles, good morals, and values that served him throughout his life, values that he learned and passed onto his children. Even in the end, Tom was concerned about how Betty would get along financially after he died. Tom rarely thought about himself. He died August 7, 1987.

And Then There Were Ten

Janet Lilburn Loker

Janet

One year, ten months, two days older than Adele, Janet Lilburn Loker was born August 14, 1926. She was beautiful, even for a young girl, and quite popular. She, like her siblings, attended Holy Name School and Sophie Wright High School.

Janet was remembered as having a hard time with sibling relationships because of her birth order. She would pick on Adele unmercifully because she was jealous and no longer in the spotlight as the "baby."

Adele recalls,

> We were walking home from Holy Name School after the Christmas party. I remember bringing gifts to some of my friends but I did not receive one present from any of them. Janet and I were walking together and she had an arm full of presents. I asked Janet if she would let me help her carry some of the presents home, but she just said "No." I was

just embarrassed and didn't want Mother and Daddy to see me with no presents. Janet went inside to show Mother all of her presents. I just stayed outside and played until dark because I did not want Mother to see me with no presents.

Janet's resentment of Adele continued for years.
Janet had a good figure and was quite a dancer. The dance gene is a strong one in the Loker family, and Janet had it. She was also apparently a fun date—she would be booked three weeks in advance. While she had the dancing and dating down pat, she was not as successful in her marriages. She was married four times. She married Donald Coleman for four years and was divorced by 1950.

After her divorce from Coleman, Janet dropped all of her friends and associated with a completely different crowd none of the family knew. She began drinking more. Mere said that was a silent cross for her. With tremendous strength and determination, Janet became interested in politics and ran for public office. However, she lost the race for the House of Representatives. Representing the 12th Ward, Janet (Davidson at the time) ran as #31 for the Democratic Party on the slogan, "A woman's place is in the House." Her platform read as follows:

1. Active volunteer in the campaign of the late "Chep" Morrison.

2. Outspoken advocate of good government measures on municipal and state levels.

3. Will initiate and support legislation to expand LSUNO.

4. Implement legislation to upgrade elementary and secondary education in New Orleans.

5. Supports teacher pay raises.

6. Favors constitutional convention to update archaic constitution.

7. Will oppose any increase in present tax structure.

8. Will fight for fair share of tax monies for Orleans Parish from the State.

Today's ballots are much the same, indicating that very little has changed in all these years. Janet liked people and had a million friends. She was constantly hosting Bingo parties for which the proceeds would go to help a poor family or someone in need.

In 1954, Janet married Banks Barbee and together in 1959, they had a daughter Brenda Loker Barbee, who lived only four days. They had a second child, Janet, whom she named after herself. Both Janets were devoted to each other.

Later, Janet had trouble paying the rent, and she and little Janet ended up living in an apartment with Mere. Mere tried her best to be a grounded and positive influence in the young child's life. It was a difficult time for everyone. Janet had two other unsuccessful marriages after Barbee. One was to David Davidson and the other to Gene Robichaux. Little Janet later died at the age of thirty of a drug overdose.

When any of the nieces and nephews came to visit, Janet was gracious and warm and always glad to see them, usually with a cigarette in one hand and sometimes a drink in the other. In a deep, raspy voice, she would welcome everyone. Janet was the third adult child to be living back with Mere.

When Janet was in the hospital with cancer, she would not let anyone visit her. Myra had died, Kathleen did not have a car, Babydoll at that time lived in Gulfport, Sister had moved to Poplarville, and Adele was the only one left. Finally, Janet agreed to let Adele pick her up from the hospital and bring Janet to her house for dinner. Gradually, Janet softened. It has been suggested that possibly Janet was looking for a better relationship with the sister she had treated so badly for years. Daughter Janet was married to Billy Hadley by then, and maybe Janet did not want to be alone. Whatever the reason, Janet made a connection with Adele. Both were able to let go of their differences. At the end of Janet's illness, Adele called the ambulance to take her to the hospital. Kathleen and little Janet met her at Touro Infirmary. Adele started praying and held her hand. Janet died very peacefully. At last, the two sisters were reconciled.

Some members of the family have labeled Janet "the black sheep" based on her drinking and unsuccessful four marriages. However, she seemed like a troubled soul who was desperately looking for her place in life. She was talented and popular. She knew and loved her roots, but she was restless and rebellious. She had been through a lot. She told Adele she had been through forty operations in her lifetime. It must not have been easy being number nine in a family of ten. She relinquished her place as the baby, and she was preceded by a long list of strong personalities. Some family members believe Janet was lost in the shuffle and was possibly depressed. No one will ever know for sure, but it is clear that she did love her daughter and her family very much. She died March 12, 1983.

Laura Adele Marie Penrose Loker Hughs (Adele)

Adele

On June 16, 1928, Mere and Pere's last child was born. They named her Laura Adele Penrose Loker. Tall and dark-haired with dark brown eyes, Adele talked about her childhood with great love. While living on Calhoun Street when she was six years old, Adele would wait for Pere at the streetcar line and walk home with him. After he retired in his early fifties, he was able to spend more time with her, and they spent many hours together. Adele also loved to swing swings in Audubon Park. She would walk to Loyola through the arcade to the side door of Holy Name Church. In those days, the church doors were always open. She would sit there for hours staring at the stained glass windows. When she was older, she would get up very early in the morning to pick figs and Japanese plums in Mr. Gladney's yard, conveniently located on LaSalle Street around the corner from the Lokers.

Adele remembered when she was four years old, she accidentally broke a drinking glass of Mere's. Crying and scared, she cleaned up the mess she had made on the floor. Eleven-year old-George, who from an early age valued honesty, walked into the room, so she explained her dilemma and he cautioned her to tell the truth, always the best policy. When Mere lined up all ten children to uncover the culprit, Adele admitted her mistake but got spanked anyway. However, George was there to comfort her and emphasize that she had done the right thing.

Realizing an empty nest was around the corner, Mere would often keep Adele and Janet home to keep her company. That would never be allowed today. When Adele was seven or eight, Mere's sister Carrie would pick her up in her chauffeur-driven Packard and take Adele swimming at the New Orleans Country Club. They had lunch, always a BLT sandwich and a milkshake, and then Max, the chauffeur, would drive her home. Aunt Carrie and Uncle Leon continued to have lunch with Adele on Saturdays until they moved to Tucson, where Adele would later spend time with them.

Adele was registered to attend the Academy of the Sacred Heart, but at the last minute, she panicked and refused to go. The nun in charge, Sister Clothilde, told Adele that God would hold her responsible for everything she learned. So, as most literal six-year-olds reason, she thought she could fool God. In her mind, if she learned nothing, he would not hold her responsible. Adele ended up going to Holy Name and Sophie Wright School with Janet. Later, she attended Loyola and Tulane University for a while, the Cox Communication school in Arizona, and Soulé

Business College. Adele did not fool God after all. She was much smarter than she previously thought.

With her siblings gone from the house, at eighteen, Adele modeled and worked downtown at Kreeger's dress store and became the character "Barbara Barlcay," the personal shopper for the store. At one of the style shows, store owner Harvey Kreeger served martinis, to which Adele must have been allergic. After breaking out in red splotches, she vowed it was her first and last martini.

While Adele worked as a secretary for Mike O'Leary at the St. Charles Hotel, she had the thrill of her life when she got comedian Bob Hope's autograph. She had a crush on Hope since the seventh grade. He gave Adele two front row tickets to his show, and during the performance, he winked at her. She kept scrapbooks of him for years.

Later, Adele worked as a secretary for the Medical and Surgical Specialties at the LSU Medical School and, later, the Marathon Corporation. In 1953, she was transferred to Atlanta. After all of Mere's children were gone, Mere and Adele had lived together. Mere had become very dependent on Adele. With a good deal of emotion on both parts and the encouragement from family friend Father Hardy to pursue this opportunity to be independent, Adele ventured to Atlanta with the help of friend Jeanne Ory.

On the ride to Georgia, Adele had a blowout in Tuscaloosa, Alabama. With no spare cash, she gave a carton of cigarettes that she found on the car seat to a truck load of convicts as payment for fixing her flat tire. Later, she wondered how the cigarettes got in her car because Jeanne had just gotten out of the convent and Adele did not smoke. "All I can say is God is good."

After Adele got settled in Atlanta, she began a routine of daily mass before work, a church visit on her lunch hour, and novenas three nights a week after work. To please Mere, Adele called cousin Laura Smith, who wanted to give Adele a cocktail party to meet all the eligible bachelors in Atlanta. When the doorbell rang the night of the party, Adele thought it was the chauffeur to pick her up. Instead, it was her escort for the evening, Billy Hughs, who would become the light of her life. Mere said later that Bill Hughs was the only man created for Adele. In 1955, Adele and Bill married. In 1959, they moved from Atlanta to Jackson, Mississippi, and in 1966, they moved to New Orleans. During those years, they produced Myra, Billy, Semmes, and Susan.

Bill was outgoing and worked in the insurance business. (Both Billy and Semmes work in the insurance business now.) Bill was also an incredible dancer and, being very tall, he and Adele made quite a pair on the dance floor. They had a wonderful marriage that lasted sixteen years, until Bill's death from liver cancer July 16, 1971. Adele then went to work, holding four jobs to support her family. She was manager of the Stratford Club, while also working at Loyola University and later, Tulane University. Adele's secretarial skills made it possible for three of her children to go free to Tulane University at the same time. She worked for pennies for tuition waivers. In between jobs, Adele found time to meet with Father Harold Cohen on Loyola's campus to help form the Catholic Pentecostal Group, which grew into the Catholic Charismatic Renewal of New Orleans. She was also responsible for starting the Perpetual Adoration Chapel at Holy Name of Jesus church and maintaining its attendance seven days a week, twenty-four hours a day, oftentimes taking for herself the slots no one else wanted.

After Bill died, Adele's brother George became more than just an uncle to the children. Living only two doors away, he spent time with the children on a daily basis at his sister's house. He acted as a surrogate father to meet their needs and gave moral support to Adele. George was a kind, genteel man, not unlike Bill Hughs, and he helped to fill a huge void in the family's lives.

Adele's commitment to her religion was unwavering and a source of consolation. She spent her life helping people in any way she could. Often this included listening to and/or praying with others. "She had the gift of making others see their own talents and gifts," writes daughter Susan. A couple of Adele's siblings, Walmsley and Kathleen, spent their dying days in her converted living room. She not only felt close to her family, but loved and was loyal to each and every one of them. Most of the family feels that she had a direct line to Heaven and was always engaging his help. She was always there for her nieces and nephews and anyone else in need. If anyone had a crisis or a simple problem, Adele used her best weapon—prayer—a gift that strengthened her throughout her life.

Adele admitted that she was disorganized and hated housework with a passion. She was, however, a wonderful cook. Cheese straws and sausage biscuits were her specialties, and in later years, they were distributed to local stores under the label "Adele's Delicacies." She later suffered from neuropathy, making it difficult for her to stand up for any length of time in the kitchen. Her gifts of delicacies were even more coveted.

Daughter Susan muses Adele's words, "Unconditional, unwavering love, and Adele's exaggerated pride in the undisputed perfection and brilliance of her awesomely, wonderful, gifted, talented, beautiful children. With other people, these adjectives reflect mere opinions, but when they applied to her own offspring, these adjectives and adverbs represent FACTS."

Susan continues to describe her mother's ability to get the job done on the premise that a person attracts bees with honey. "She parks whenever she wants, strangers put gas in her car at self-serve pumps, and the list goes on. I know of no woman for whom that sugary, Southern damsel-in-distress 'I just don't know how to . . . could you please help me, Sugarfoot?' routine worked as well. The fact is that it was hard to turn Adele down. Adele died October 9, 2015.

Adele

And Then There Were Ten

Howard Loker Black

Howard Black

Howard Black, Pere's nephew, was Mere and Pere's unofficially adopted son. Aunt Emma, Pere's sister, died when Howard was six years old. His father died when he was fifteen. Mrs. Gore raised Howard after his parents died but also felt there was such an age difference between herself and the boy that perhaps it would be better for Howard to be in a loving family environment. She asked Mere to adopt Howard, and Mere agreed. In 1933, Mere and Pere went to the train station to meet Howard, who was a junior in high school at the time. Mere had a party for him at the house to make him feel welcomed. Howard was incredibly handsome with beautiful blond hair. Howard and Brother hit it off more than the others, and the two ended up rooming together.

In Howard's senior year at Jesuit, he came home and told Mere that he registered for the draft. Mere was upset and tried to explain the importance of finishing his education. However, the war was going on and Howard felt the obligation to serve. A few weeks later, he got the call, informing him of his acceptance into the draft. He was trained as a pilot in the Army Air Corps. During his two weeks of basic training, he met Francis Walmsley (no relation) as a part of the USO. After a whirlwind two-week courtship, she asked Howard to marry her and he did, to the disappointment of Mere and Pere. Within less than one month of their marriage, Howard was killed by enemy jets. Francis later told the family that she never loved Howard and got Howard's allotment (it was said she felt she did not deserve his allotment and gave it to Mere). She was never seen again. He died January 2, 1944.

Howard Black

Prologue

What I learned from writing this book is that no matter how many times people change, the one quintessential factor that is constant is the love of family.

The history of the Loker children reminds me of the same changes that the Monarch butterflies endure. In both cases the results are beautiful.

Prologue

Mere and her six girls (left to right) Janet, Mimi, Kitty, Myra, Mere, Babydoll, Adele

MASS MEETING!

All good citizens are invited to attend a mass meeting on SATURDAY, March 14, at 10 o'clock a. m., at Clay Statue, to take steps to remedy the failure of justice in the HENNESSY CASE. Come prepared for action.

John C. Wickliffe,
B. F. Glover,
J. G. Pepper,
C. E. Rogers,
F. E. Hawes,
Raymond Hayes,
L. E. Cenas,
John M. Parker, Jr.,
Harris B. Lewis,
Septime Villere,
Wm. M. Railey,
Lee McMillan,
C. E. Jones,
J. F. Queeny,
D. R. Calder,
Thomas Henry,
James Lea McLean,
Felix Couturie,
T. D. Wharton,
Frank B. Hayne,
J. G. Flower,
James Clarke,
Thomas H. Kelley,
R. B. Ogden,
Ulric Atkinson,
A. Baldwin, Jr,
A. E. Blackmar,
John V. Moore,
Wm. T. Pierson,
O. L. Stogal,
E. T. Leche.

W. S. Parkerson,
Henry Dickson Bruns,
Wm. H. Deeves,
Richard S. Venables,
Samuel B. Merwin,
Omer Villere,
H. L. Favrot,
T. D. Mather,
James P. Mulvey,
Emile Dupre,
W. P. Curtiss,
Chas. J. Hanlett,
T. S. Barton,
C. J. Forstall,
J. Moore Wilson,
Hugh W. Brown,
C. Harrison Parker,
Edgar H. Farrar,
J. C. Aby,
Rud. Hahse,
C. A. Walecker,
W. Mosby,
Chas. M. Barnwell,
H. R. Labouisse,
Walter D. Denegre,
George Denegre,
R. H. Hornbeck,
S. P. Walmsley,
E. H. Pierson,
James D. Houston.

Appendix

Thomas Jenkins Semmes, Sylvester Pierce Walmsley, And "Who Killa Da Chief"

T. Semmes Favrot
October 2024

Thomas J. Semmes, grandfather of Mere (Myra Walmsley Loker) and his son-in-law, Sylvester Pierce Walmsley, Mere's father, were both deeply intertwined with the complex and tumultuous events surrounding the assassination of New Orleans Police Chief David Hennessy in 1890, as well as the ensuing trials and lynchings that followed. David Hennessy was known for his aggressive stance against crime and corruption in New Orleans, particularly against the city's growing Mafia problem. The Mafia arrived in New Orleans from Italy with the city's large and growing Italian immigrant population. The local Mafia started out committing petty crimes mostly among local Italian immigrants, but eventually their criminal activities began to grow and spread. Hennessy set out to eliminate the Mafia problem via tough policing, with considerable success. On October 15, 1890, he was shot and killed while walking home in the evening, an act that sent shockwaves through the city and across the nation. Mere was two years old at the time.

The local police arrested eleven suspected mafiosi who were charged with Hennessy's murder. In the course of preparing for their trial, representatives of the accused approached prominent local attorney Thomas J. Semmes, one of the deans of the local bar, seeking to hire him as part of the defense team. Semmes was not really interested in taking on the case, so he quoted an exorbitant fee as the cost of his participation. The accused were supposedly poor immigrants who worked as fruit peddlers and in similar blue-collar jobs, so Semmes assumed they would never be able to pay his quoted fee. Much to his surprise, these ostensibly poor working-class immigrants immediately agreed to pay his fee, so he was hired, though not as lead counsel for the defense. Rather, he appeared at trial and conducted some of the arguments on behalf of the defense, it being thought that the presence of this distinguished jurist would help sway the jury toward an acquittal.

The trial took place in March 1891 and drew considerable local and national public attention. Despite overwhelming evidence, through blatant jury tampering and bribery, the defendants were acquitted. The acquittal sparked outrage across the city and the country, and the local mafiosi openly bragged that the Mafia would soon rule New Orleans.

The day after the acquittal, on March 14, 1891, a notice was published in the New Orleans Times-Picayune inviting citizens to a mass meeting at the Henry Clay statue on Canal Street, the same place from which the Battle of Liberty Place was launched in 1874, and the favorite spot for such "mass meetings" in the days before mass communication. The notice was signed by "61 of New Orleans' most prominent citizens," including Sylvester Pierce Walmsley, who had become Thomas J. Semmes' son-in-law five years earlier upon marrying Mamee (Myra Eulalie Semmes) in 1885. Walmsley had also reigned as Rex the year before, in 1890. The notice, a copy of which is attached, invited people to come to the meeting "to take steps to remedy the failure of justice in the Hennessy case. Come prepared for action." At the mass meeting, the signers of the notice made speeches to the large crowd. Then a selected group of the signers led the crowd and "formed ranks and marched to a Canal St. gun-store, where they armed themselves with rifles and shotguns." They then stormed the Orleans Parish Prison, located near where Armstrong Park is now located, and killed eleven of the acquitted mafiosi (nine were shot and two were hanged, on the spot).

After the lynching, the Italian government expressed outrage and concern. They viewed the lynching as a serious affront to their citizens living in the United States. The Italian government demanded justice and broke off diplomatic relations with the U.S., stoking fears of war. In response to Italy's concerns, the U.S. government took several steps to address the diplomatic crisis. Secretary of State James G. Blaine communicated with the Italian government, emphasizing the need for legal process and expressing condolences for the loss of life. The U.S. government assured Italy that it would investigate the incidents surrounding the lynching and that it was committed to upholding the rule of law. Despite these assurances, no investigation of the lynching was ever made and no one was ever prosecuted for it. The local and national press and public opinion were all supportive of what they saw as justice being served after the corrupt manipulation of the justice system by the Mafia. Thus, the broader tensions between the United States and Italy persisted for some time.

However, in order to defuse the crisis, a naive federal government paid compensation to the families of the eleven lynched mafiosi. This money is said to have been seized by the Mafia and used as seed money to jump-start their criminal enterprise to a higher level. Thus, contrary to popular belief, the American Mafia got its start in New Orleans, rather than New York or elsewhere.

Appendix

So, Thomas J. Semmes helped get the mafiosi acquitted, and immediately after the acquittal, his son-in-law S. P. Walmsley became part of a group that convened a mass meeting, which then formed a lynch mob that shot and hanged the mafiosi that Semmes had just helped get acquitted. Oh, to have been a fly on the wall when father-in-law and son-in-law next ran into each other! Notably, neither Mere nor my grandmother Kathleen Loker Gibbons ("Kitty") ever told me this story. I feel pretty certain that the family likely sought to bury the story and keep it from succeeding generations. Mere may not have even known about it; as noted, she was two years old when it happened.

The story wasn't completely buried, however. After I discovered the Hennessy story and Semmes' and Walmsley's connection to it, I asked my uncle, Jack Gibbons, if he knew anything about all of this. He told me that when he was young one of his Loker uncles (I can't remember which one) once discussed the Hennessy assassination with him and proudly told Jack that his grandfather (i.e., S. P. Walmsley) was one of the men who had "remedied the failure of justice" by eliminating the acquitted mafiosi.

It is unknown whether in fact S. P. Walmsley was actually directly involved with the lynching at Parish Prison. It was apparently agreed at the outset that only a select subset of the sixty-one men who signed the call to the mass meeting would actually proceed to lead the lynch mob to the prison. The identity of those men was never revealed, not out of fear of prosecution, but out of fear of retaliation by the Mafia.

The events surrounding Hennessy's assassination, the subsequent trial, and the lynching of the accused left a lasting impact on New Orleans. For generations afterward, New Orleans schoolchildren were known to taunt their Italian-American counterparts with cries of "Who killa da chief?"

Myra is an enthusiast who enjoy bridge, the arts, gardening, dance, travel, chocolate, and anything creative. She has three sons and six grandchildren and is a die hard New Orleanian who has spent a large part of her life enjoying the benefits of Audubon Park. She credits her Sacred Heart education for her love of writing. This is her first book.